Praise for *Simply Effective*

"*Simply Effective* is a call to action. In our increasingly complex business world, we need to constantly find ways to simplify the way we do things. Ashkenas draws on his vast experience as a consultant to give us a practical and straightforward roadmap for simplification."

> —Andreas Fibig, Chairman of the Board of Management,
> Bayer Schering Pharma AG

"Overcoming complexity is *the* management challenge of the twenty-first century and for the financial services industry in particular. If you don't want complexity to become as inevitable as death and taxes (with similar consequences) you need to read this book. Ron Ashkenas has a unique ability to cut through the clutter and help you focus on what's important."

> —Peter R. Fisher, Managing Director and Co-Head of Fixed
> Income Portfolio Managment Group, BlackRock

"If there is any institution that suffers from complexity overload, it's a hospital. Some of that complexity is unavoidable—but much of it is of our own creation. Ashkenas challenges us to not accept this complexity as a given, but to do something about it. Reading his book is a good way to start."

> —Martha H. Marsh, President and CEO, Stanford Hospital
> and Clinics

"I've always said that 'simplicity is the next frontier of productivity.' Ron Ashkenas knows just how to put that quote into practice—and that's what this book is about."

> —Gary Rodkin, CEO, ConAgra Foods

Simply
Effective

Simply Effective

How to Cut Through Complexity in Your
Organization and Get Things Done

Ron Ashkenas

Harvard Business Press

Boston, Massachusetts

Copyright 2010 Harvard Business School Publishing Corporation
All rights reserved
Printed in the United States of America
14 13 12 11 10   5 4 3 2 1

Library of Congress Cataloging-in-Publication Data

Ashkenas, Ronald N.
    Simply effective : how to cut through complexity in your organization and get
things done / Ron Ashkenas.
        p. cm.
    Includes bibliographical references.
    ISBN 978-1-4221-8114-0 (hbk. : alk. paper) 1.   Organizational effectiveness.
2.   Organizational change. 3.   Organizational behavior. 4.   Management.
I.   Title.
    HD58.9.A84 2009
    658—dc22

                                                                    2009021139

The paper used in this publication meets the requirements of the American
National Standard for Permanence of Paper for Publications and Documents in
Libraries and Archives Z39.48-1992.

Simply
Effective

How to Cut Through Complexity in Your
Organization and Get Things Done

Ron Ashkenas

Harvard Business Press

Boston, Massachusetts

Copyright 2010 Harvard Business School Publishing Corporation
All rights reserved
Printed in the United States of America
14 13 12 11 10   5 4 3 2 1

Library of Congress Cataloging-in-Publication Data

Ashkenas, Ronald N.
    Simply effective : how to cut through complexity in your organization and get
things done / Ron Ashkenas.
        p. cm.
    Includes bibliographical references.
    ISBN 978-1-4221-8114-0 (hbk. : alk. paper) 1.   Organizational effectiveness.
2.   Organizational change. 3.   Organizational behavior. 4.   Management.
I.   Title.
    HD58.9.A84 2009
    658—dc22

                                                                    2009021139

The paper used in this publication meets the requirements of the American
National Standard for Permanence of Paper for Publications and Documents in
Libraries and Archives Z39.48-1992.

CONTENTS

PREFACE

This book grew out of my long-standing interest in making organizations simpler and more effective. My thoughts about how to do this were first expressed in "Simplicity-Minded Management," an article I wrote for *Harvard Business Review* in 2007.[1] There, I highlighted the importance of simplifying organizations—structure, products, processes, and behaviors—so that leaders could make it easier for their people to get results and delight customers. My hope was that managers would confront the reality that much of the complexity in their organizations was self-generated and would begin to view "simplicity-mindedness" as a competence or skill that they should develop over the course of their careers.

After the article was published, I received numerous questions from managers, consultants, executives, and HR professionals asking what was *really* involved in simplification. How do you get a better understanding of where complexity is coming from? How do you deal with the different types of complexity in organizations? How can you develop a comprehensive strategy for simplification? What if you don't need to simplify everything? What can you do if you're not the CEO?

These questions led me to realize that organizations and their leaders needed more than just an appreciation of the importance of simplification—they actually needed a handbook or guide for how to go about it. So that's the intent of this book—to lay out a practical set of tools and strategies for simplifying organizations, with a focus on getting rid of the complexity that managers generate themselves.

But this isn't just a "nice to do" activity. To some extent, almost all managers today are struggling with complexity—overloaded with information without enough time to process it; juggling multiple variables without fully knowing how they might interact with each other; dealing with people from different functions, units, organizations, and geographies without being able to align their different agendas and priorities; and doing all this while being buffeted by new regulations, new technologies, uncertain markets, and changing competitive threats. It's as though managers have been placed in high-speed flight simulators with hundreds of gauges, dials, buttons, and levers—and no instruction manual or preflight training for how to fly the plane. Except it's real!

Countering all this complexity, however, is not a mechanical exercise. You can't just follow a set of how-to instructions, connect the dots, check off the boxes, and arrive at perfect simplicity. Organizations are social organisms that need to accomplish their missions in ever-changing and increasingly turbulent environments. And organizations all differ from one another in crucial ways. Leaders therefore need to create tailored simplification strategies that match the unique conditions they face, to get to the degree of simplicity that is appropriate for their situations. To do this, they have to engage their colleagues in an ongoing dialogue about the sources of complexity and their implications, and experiment with different approaches until they figure out what works. It's a learning process—and it's ongoing. The forces and sources of complexity never sleep.

Simply Effective is meant as a resource for managers, consultants, and others who want to engage in this ongoing and never-ending quest. It provides a framework for understanding the major sources of managerially generated complexity, diagnostic instruments for assessing the levels of complexity around you, and a range of tools and an overall strategy for driving toward greater simplification.

Many, if not most, of the individual tools will be familiar to readers and have been described in depth by others (and I'll point you in the right direction if you want further explanations). My intention is not to rehash these tools but rather to put them into the context of how they can be used either singly or in combination to tackle different aspects of complexity—or to be woven together into a more comprehensive strategy.

To make all this come alive, *Simply Effective* also includes examples and case studies from real organizations that have embarked on the journey toward simplification, some recently, and some over many years. Since GE was a pioneer in using simplification to drive results, a number of the examples come from that experience, including an extensive case in chapter 6 about how simplicity has become incorporated into the mind-set and culture of GE over the course of two decades. But many other organizations also provide illustrations and rich learning about what it takes to cut through complexity and get things done, and these are drawn from almost thirty years of consulting experience. While some of the cases go back a few years, the points that they illustrate are still relevant since managerially generated complexity is a timeless issue. None of the cases, though, are meant to suggest that simplification by itself is a guaranty of business success. Many other business fundamentals need to be in place—in addition to simplicity—for a company to thrive or for managers to be successful, but these lie beyond the scope of the book. However, if complexity is allowed to go unchecked, it is likely that managers will have more difficulty leveraging these other success factors. In other words, while simplicity will not guaranty success, too much complexity will certainly increase the chances of failure.

What Does Simplification Really Mean?

What do I mean by simplification? Here's a real-world example: suppose you want to drive to another town. It's not far, but you don't know the way. So you get directions—which roads to take, when to turn, key landmarks: simple. Everything is straightforward, and you reach your destination easily.

But what if your request for directions evokes a lot more information—road surface details, photos of every building along the way, a history of the area, and a few satellite maps at different scales? And what if even more information shows up while you're en route? And what if a thunderstorm blows through in the middle of your trip? And then what if construction blocks some of the roads and you have to change course, and then you have a flat tire along the way? Getting things done in organizations is like getting yourself from one town to another. Sometimes it's like that first trip. But more often than not, it's like the second: you have to sort through lots of potentially relevant information in advance, deal with real-time data, respond to changing conditions, make decisions on the fly, and generally work hard to get where you want to go. And that assumes that you actually know where you are going and that your companions are content to let you make all the choices about how to get there—which, of course, is rarely the case. In other words, getting things done in organizations is usually far from simple.

If you are running an organization, you can accept this complexity as a given—something you just have to live with. Or you can do something about it and make your workplace simpler, more productive, and more satisfying for customers and employees. That's

what simplification means—making it easier for your people to get things done and for your customers and other partners to work with you. If you want to take that path, then this book is for you.

Journey to Simplicity

My first encounter with simplicity as a business issue was at GE in 1989. At the time, I was part of the consulting team that then-CEO Jack Welch had assembled to transform the company from a slow-moving, bureaucratic, top-down, overly analytical organization to one that would be fast, flexible, and boundaryless. As we developed what became known as the GE Work-Out process to accomplish this transformation, simplicity emerged as one of the key goals of the effort. In Welch's view, speed and simplicity were intertwined—and both were critical for GE's success. To move faster and be more responsive to customers and to markets, GE would have to reduce the number of steps required to get things done and make it easier for everyone to understand how to take those steps. Consequently, a lot of the resulting projects focused on simplifying processes, both internally and externally. But simplicity at GE was more than just process streamlining—it was a mind-set and a culture that eventually permeated the way managers organized and led the company.

Perhaps because of GE's high-profile success, many other companies subsequently adopted simplicity as a core value, or an aspiration to strive toward. Others picked it up as their business environments became more complex or global or competitive (or as they saw other firms doing so). But very few companies acted like they knew what simplicity really meant, or how to make it drive business results. In fact, it seemed that many organizations just wanted to copy GE's tools for simplification (such as Work-Out and Six Sigma) but didn't understand that simplicity was more than just a set of projects.

As I saw attempt after attempt to simplify meet with disappointment or outright failure, I realized that most managers were not addressing simplification as a skill or a mind-set or a core competence of leadership (which was how it was understood at GE). This is what prompted me to write the *HBR* article.

This insight has only been reinforced by the global financial crisis that began in 2007, much of which was triggered by complexity so baroque that it compromised the ability of financial, governmental, and commercial institutions to manage risk safely and appropriately. For example, here's how the *New York Times* described one cause of the sub-subprime mortgage crisis:

> The confusion about these products lies in part in their complexity. Structured products are pooled assets that have been sliced and diced into ever smaller, more specialized pieces . . . Banks and other financial institutions pooled those asset-backed securities into new units, dividing them up again and issuing securities against them, creating collateralized debt obligations [C.D.O.'s]. The idea took off, with new combinations that were further removed from the original asset. New creations included C.D.O.'s of C.D.O.'s, called C.D.O.-squared. There is even a C.D.O.-cubed.[2]

In addition to the complexity of their products, many financial firms that collapsed and were either shut down or bailed out also suffered from fragmented and complex risk-management processes that left them unable to identify risk issues until it was too late and from financial processes that kept them from fully accounting for their products and liabilities. These further complexities embarrassed the CEOs, who had to restate their losses or potential liabilities numerous times—conveying the (unfortunately, quite correct) impression that they did not have the situation under control. Perhaps most disconcerting about the subprime episode and

subsequent market implosion was the extent to which it illustrated everyone's lack of understanding of the complex interdependencies between financial institutions, other commercial establishments, government regulators and central banks, and the world economy.

Despite our recent economic struggles, the global economy is not going to get less complex. If anything, it will grow more difficult to understand. In addition, the pace of technological innovation and breakthrough will continue to increase, which will also add to complexity. It's as though Thomas Friedman's "flat world" has met Alvin Toffler's "future shock," and the resulting explosion has made everything incredibly complex.[3] As a result many executives and managers feel that their organizations are becoming ungovernable, unwieldy, and tangled in knots.

But while dramatic (and traumatic) situations such as the demise of Lehman Brothers or the end of traditional investment banking garner all the publicity, the bigger challenge is that many managers are feeling overwhelmed by complexity on a day-to-day basis. As a result, managers are working longer hours with greater stress, and feeling less and less productive. They attend meetings, sort through e-mail and voice mail, travel around the globe, manage relationships with dozens of people inside and outside their organizations—and at the end of the day often don't feel they have accomplished very much. And they worry that perhaps they are contributing to or creating the next financial scandal or subprime meltdown. This is the true crisis of complexity that is facing us all.

But it doesn't have to be this way. While much complexity is caused by globalization and advances in technology and a host of other external trends, perhaps an equal amount is caused by the way we structure our organizations, design our products and services, construct our business processes, and manage our people. As Scott Adams, the creator of the *Dilbert* cartoons, humorously points out, senior managers often turn their organizations into what he calls "confusopolies."[4] But as a manager and leader, you have a choice. Either you can add to complexity and make things more confusing, or you can simplify work and make it easier for people to get things done. My objective here is to give you a resource guide for how to choose the latter.

Structure of the Book

Since this book is about simplicity, I've tried to make it simple to navigate. Chapter 1 starts with a definition of simplicity and its importance, and then provides illustrations of how combating complexity can make a significant difference in getting things done. The chapter then introduces the four ways that managers unintentionally create complexity in their organizations—through structure, products, processes, and their own behaviors—and a road map of the tools that will be presented throughout the book for overcoming these sources of complexity. Included in chapter 1 is a brief questionnaire that will allow you to diagnose which of these areas might be of most concern for your organization.

Chapters 2 through 5, the heart of the book, tackle each of the four causes of complexity in depth—including the traps that managers fall into and what you can do to avoid them. Each of these chapters also focuses on specific and practical tools that you can use to foster simplicity in that particular area.

The final two chapters show how the various tools and approaches can be combined into an integrated strategy. Chapter 6 outlines an ongoing company- or divisionwide strategy for simplification that senior executives can employ to drive improved results both in the short term and over time. Chapter 7 describes a more individual strategy for how you can foster simplicity in your own work and with your immediate colleagues—no matter what your role in the organization.

In summary, this is a book about taking control of complexity—not in a rigid and sequential or an overly prescribed manner but in a way that matches the needs of your organization and your level of influence and authority. In the final analysis, nobody else is going to make your workplace easier and simpler and more productive. It's up to you. I hope this book will give you a helping hand.

Acknowledgments

Although this is the first book that I've written by myself, it was certainly not a solo effort. Many others provided both material and emotional support, without which this book would not have taken shape.

First and foremost are the many talented managers who realized that *simplicity* was not just a nice word on a corporate value statement, but an imperative for success. Their stories make up a large portion of this book. But more importantly, what I learned from them helped me formulate the insights that I've tried to capture here. I've been fortunate over the years to have worked with many capable and thoughtful executives, all of whom have shared their wisdom with me. This book would not have been possible without them. In particular, I'd like to acknowledge Pete Perez, executive vice president of human resources at ConAgra Foods, and John Lynch, senior vice president of corporate human resources at General Electric, for their assistance. In addition, I want to thank Larry DeMonaco, retired vice president of human resources at GE Capital, for his thoughtful review of the draft manuscript.

My colleagues at Robert H. Schaffer & Associates were also instrumental in the development of this book, providing me with the time to do it and the encouragement to keep going when I got discouraged. Many of the tools presented in *Simply Effective* were created or enhanced by members of the firm, and many of the cases come from our practice. So, in many ways, this book is really a product of the pioneering work that RHS&A has done for the past fifty years. In particular, Robert Schaffer read many early chapter drafts and offered helpful feedback, as did Wes Siegal. Also at RHS&A, Katie Beavan, Matthew McCreight, Keith Michaelson, Patrice Murphy, and Rick Heinick provided case material; Michel Nabti conducted very useful secondary research; Sarah Larson helped organize the cases; Cindy DeCarlo, Amy Beebe, and Maura Pratt provided administrative support; and Joanne Young kept me organized throughout the year of writing. Colleagues and friends from other firms also contributed material and encouragement and include Marian Powell from Korn Consulting Group, Bob Kaplan from Kaplan-DeVries, and Dave Ulrich from RBL. Thanks to all for your help and support.

This book would not have seen the light of day without superb editorial assistance. Ellen Peebles, senior editor of *Harvard Business Review,* helped me shape the original HBR article upon which *Simply Effective* is based. Hilary Powers guided me through the process of transforming thousands of words into a coherent and increasingly simple manuscript. Melinda Merino of the Harvard Business Press then pushed me to sharpen and further simplify the manuscript so that it would be a readable and hopefully useful book. Although I take final accountability—for better or for worse—for the end product, much of the credit for the final shape of the book goes to them.

Since book writing is not my day job, *Simply Effective* consumed many evenings and weekends over the past year. This required patience and understanding from my family members, all of whom took time out of their own busy lives to support and encourage my writing. Thanks to my children, Eli, Elie, Shira, Ari, and Rebecca; and new grandson, Noam (who will have a lot to chew on with this book). Even more thanks are due to my wife, Barbara, whose newly empty nest was even emptier at times when I was preoccupied with this book. I couldn't have done this without your support.

A Final Word: Simplicity Can Make a Difference

As I write this preface, the world is in the throes of perhaps the worst recession in thirty years. The financial system has melted down and is being transformed; the automobile industry is reeling; retail organizations are struggling to survive; public service and health-care institutions are overwhelmed; governments around the world are pumping huge amounts of money into their economies and running up unprecedented deficits; and stock market plunges have wiped out trillions of dollars in personal wealth and shaken many people's confidence in their future security. As if this weren't enough, governments are also struggling to develop renewable energy sources, reduce global warming, protect their citizens against terrorism, and bring billions of people out of poverty. It's a daunting time for organizations of all kinds, public and private, throughout the world.

Yet at the same time, we are in the midst of the greatest technological revolution in human history. Advances in travel, telecommunication, and computing have made it possible to shrink the world and create a truly global economy. The mapping of the human genome holds the promise of reducing and preventing disease. Developments in physics, nanotechnology, and material sciences are transforming manufacturing while new approaches to water, food sciences, and energy hold the promise of freeing us from traditional resource constraints. In other words, despite the doom and gloom of the global economy, it also is possible that we are about to enter a golden age of global prosperity that may solve many of the problems that we consider the most intractable today.

Unfortunately, none of us have the luxury of sitting back and waiting for the right combination of technical, scientific, and social breakthroughs that will get us to the golden age. We have to deal with present realities. As a consequence, we need to redouble our efforts to get the most out of our current organizations so that they can invest in new technology, experiment with new approaches, and perhaps accelerate the discoveries that will change the world. In order to do this, we need to get back to basics—to simplify structures, products, and processes; reduce clutter and wasted time; and make everyone feel as if he or she is truly contributing and not just churning on a giant gerbil wheel. Workers at all levels—from the factory floor to the public school classroom to the executive suite—want to be as productive as possible and experience a direct line of sight between their efforts and their organization's results. Our job as organizational leaders, consultants, and advisers is to help them make that happen. Simplification is not the only answer—but it's a good place to start.

—Ron Ashkenas
Stamford, Connecticut
March 2009

ONE

Unmasking Organizational Complexity

TRYING TO GET THINGS DONE in organizations today often feels like walking in quicksand. If you are a manager or an executive who is anxious to get results, you know what I mean. There are too many meetings, too many reports, too much information, and too many stakeholders—all of whom have different views on what should be done and how. Processes don't work or take too long. Decisions are delayed or unclear. Presentations go on forever. And the boundaries between home and work, online and offline, have broken down with e-mails and cell phones and 24/7 availability. Complexity is out of control and getting worse—and it compromises our ability to be effective.

But we have no one to blame but ourselves. While some complexity inevitably comes from globalization, technological advances, and regulatory requirements, much of the day-to-day complexity that bogs down our ability to get results is self-inflicted.

We create organization structures that have too many levels, redundant functions, and unclear roles. We add products, features, and services without reducing the overall portfolio of offerings or streamlining the support requirements. We build processes with too many steps and loops and missing metrics, and then don't manage them as they evolve and grow. And then we compound this complexity by giving vague assignments, not holding people accountable, miscommunicating, and avoiding conflict. The quicksand of complexity is of our own making.

But this is nothing new. Throughout human history, simplicity has been one of the "great virtues." Almost every society—Eastern, Western, ancient, and modern—has included simplicity in its principles for the good life. Indeed, the search for simplicity has been one of the few universals, bridging culture, religion, geography, and time. But perhaps the reason that so many have aspired to simplicity is that it is so difficult to achieve. And this is particularly true in organizations today. Like crabgrass in an otherwise well-manicured lawn, complexity insinuates itself into even the most well-managed organizations. And unless you have a strategy to combat it, complexity can grow and flourish despite your efforts to uproot the individual shoots.

How Complexity Creeps In

A number of years ago, I was consulting to the GE Lighting business in Cleveland. The issue was product development—how to make it faster and more effective. At the time, GE Lighting had a dominant share of the U.S. lighting market, but was in a global battle with Philips Electronics, Siemens, and other manufacturers for worldwide market share. According to John Opie, GE Lighting's president at the time, better product development was essential because the core light bulb business (they called them "lamps") was becoming increasingly commoditized and it was getting harder and harder to maintain margins solely by squeezing costs. Instead, the company needed new consumer and commercial products that could command higher prices.

It sounded simple and straightforward. But somehow, it wasn't happening fast enough.

Over the next several weeks, I learned that Opie and his team had indeed taken several steps to improve product development. They had increased investment and added more product development teams, they had instituted a formal stage-gate process to make sure that products were progressing in a disciplined manner, and they had clearly communicated to the entire organization the vital importance of new products. So what was missing?

When we brought a number of product development teams together, some answers started to emerge. First of all, because of specialized expertise, most team members were working on more than one project to meet the increased demand. The fragmentation of time was making it difficult for key people to focus and bring tasks to completion. In addition, the stage-gate process, while bringing discipline to development, was also bringing lots of extra reviews. The whole GE Lighting organization had recently shifted from a business unit model to a functional model, and each function (engineering, manufacturing, sales, marketing, international, finance, HR, and others) was conducting its own reviews to make sure that the teams were progressing toward the agreed-upon gates. One of the project teams estimated that its members were spending almost 75 percent of their time preparing for review meetings, sitting in review meetings, or responding to issues raised in review meetings. That left little enough time for actual project work. But even worse, because of the increased attention and scrutiny on product development, senior managers were constantly asking for detailed status and progress updates between the various reviews, and that was taking even more time away from real development. What was meant to be a simple process had become enormously complex.

As a result of the effort, several of these issues were addressed, and GE Lighting's product development process got a big boost. But that's not the point of this story.

My real point is that complexity does not happen all on its own. Some of it does, but managers add to it significantly. The accretion is not intentional, not conscious, not malicious. But complexity creeps in all the time. In GE Lighting's case, the extra reviews, the fragmentation of experts' time, the increased reporting and analysis—all were caused by well-meaning management actions. These complexity factors combined to make it harder to crank out new products.

But this insight includes some good news, and this good news is at the heart of this book: if managers can add complexity through unconscious actions, they can reduce it through conscious ones. The purpose of this book is to help you develop your own strategy for simplifying your organization, or your piece of it.

Simplicity as Competitive Advantage

Reducing complexity is not just a matter of making it easier to get things done. It also has the potential to drive long-term competitive advantage—not by solving every business problem—but by increasing your capacity to address issues quickly and effectively.

Take the case of Vanguard, one of the world's largest investment management companies with over one trillion dollars of assets and millions of clients around the world. Since the firm was founded in 1975, it has weathered numerous economic downturns and market crises, yet has continued to grow and thrive. In fact, in 2008, when most other financial firms were severely damaged by subprime mortgages, asset-backed securities, frozen credit markets, and capital constraints, Vanguard recorded its best year ever in winning new institutional business and had the largest inflow of new cash in the industry: same environment—different results.

Vanguard's steady and successful performance is not an accident. To a large extent, it is an outcome of the simple investing philosophy and simple operating model originally developed by its founder, John Bogle.[1] Bogle believed that investors built wealth through consistent, diversified, and straightforward investments—not through esoteric products that promised fast returns but couldn't really be explained. Vanguard calls it the "Simple Truths About Investing"—which include guidance for managing costs, being diversified, and staying the course over a long period. This philosophy led Vanguard to develop a family of no-load funds, including index funds, tax-managed funds, and other types of innovative but simple, investor-friendly vehicles. And along with a focus on credit analysis and tight risk controls, it led Vanguard to avoid investments in structured vehicles and other high-risk derivative products.

Vanguard's culture is steeped in the notion of putting the client first and thinking about how to make things easier for the client. According to Tim Buckley, managing director of Vanguard's Retail Investor Group, this is critical because the financial services industry inundates investors with so much complex jargon and so many thousands of investment choices that investors often are bewildered and consequently make uninformed decisions or throw up their hands and cede control to others. In fact, Buckley notes that Vanguard's competitors are not other investment firms, but rather "complexity and inertia." "If we can reduce or absorb complexity," he says, "we'll be able to help our customers become confident and successful investors." To do this, Vanguard limits its number of funds, makes it easy for investors to create balanced portfolios from "short lists," offers "turnkey portfolios," and is constantly searching for ways to simplify transactions or even fill out forms for the customer. In fact, Vanguard tracks not only the standard investment measures, but also clients' completion rates for transactions, which the company sees as a measure of how simple Vanguard has made it for investors to get things done.

Vanguard's operating model is also rooted in simplicity and allows the company to manage its overall infrastructure quickly and flexibly. The starting point for this simplicity is Vanguard's structure as a private, "mutualized" company in which the mutual funds own the management company, which provides services back to the funds on an at-cost basis. This keeps everyone in the company focused on maximizing investment returns and minimizing expenses since in essence the company is not trying to make a profit for anyone other than its fund investors. In this context, the company limits types of products that it supports, has a consistent and common way of accounting for financial results, and has a disciplined management process that cuts across all parts of the company. Vanguard also rotates its managers through different areas on a regular basis so that everyone is inculcated with the same operating philosophy and to prevent the development of silos that get in the way of making things happen. As Buckley notes, "If you've been in other areas and know you'll be taking on other jobs, you won't move problems downstream; you'll just solve them."

The net result of all this is that Vanguard did not fall prey to the problems of other financial services companies. And when the market fell and other companies scrambled to reduce their costs, Vanguard already had a simple, low-cost operating model—and therefore did not need to make major staff reductions. Instead, it was able to increase the amount of advice and support it provided to its investors during tough times—which made the investors even more loyal and encouraged them to continue and expand their business with Vanguard, even during a market downturn. Simplicity paid off.

Tele Atlas, an industry pioneer in digital mapping and geographic data, also used a focus on simplicity as a way of dramatically increasing its long-term value. Founded in 1984, Tele Atlas developed innovative techniques for capturing and constantly updating detailed mapping information for the growing GPS (global positioning system) market; GPS data are now common in portable navigation systems, automobiles, cell phones, and other devices. As a rapidly growing, technology-based company that needed to operate around the world, Tele Atlas benefitted from a management team that realized that simplicity was a key to success. As a result, the company evolved a standard and relatively simple way of creating and updating geographic data by having cameras installed in vans that drive through cities and on country roads taking video data of signs and landmarks, and digitally uploading them in real time to a centralized processing center.

Over time, as Tele Atlas grew and added more countries and customers, management discovered that the company was becoming more complex, inside and out. The company chief financial officer at the time, Hardie Morgan, and Jay Benson, vice president of global strategic planning, decided to simplify parts of the company where there would also be a financial payoff. They started with obvious processes such as travel and eventually evolved to areas that affect the customer. For instance, they found that product variations had multiplied and that customer-tailored applications, particularly those driven by technology, continued to add complexity. To counter this complexity, Tele Atlas created a global production platform in 2007 and worked hard to reduce the redundancy of product capabilities, the total number of products, and related process costs. In North America, for example, Tele Atlas brought together people from all its functions to develop and then successfully implement a plan for reducing the number of products by 80 percent or more in one hundred days. Products that were continued were then migrated to the global production platform. The fifty-two products that were not selected were then assigned to one of four options, depending on what would be best for their customers. The options were (1) discontinue the product; (2) switch it for one of the "migrated" products; (3) provide it as an add-on "service" to a customer; or (4) outsource it.

By taking this approach, the immediate revenue impact on Tele Atlas from discontinued products was minimal. In fact, the company retained 89 percent of the North American revenue through just eight standard products, the costs of production for which were significantly reduced. This clean profile and positioning for rapid global growth contributed to the company's attractiveness so much so that in 2008, two personal navigation companies fought to acquire it. Ultimately, Tele Atlas was purchased by TomTom for €2.9 billion. For Tele Atlas, simplicity paid off big time.

The Four Sources of Complexity in Organizations

You too can create competitive advantage by building simplicity into the way you do business—whether you are the CEO, the manager of a small team, or an individual contributor. But to start developing a simplification strategy, you need to understand the four sources of complexity in organizations (figure 1-1):

1. Structural mitosis

2. Product and service proliferation

3. Process evolution

4. Managerial behavior

FIGURE 1-1

Four sources of complexity in organizations

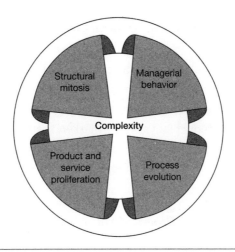

Structural Mitosis

In many ways, organizations are like living organisms.[2] Units grow, divide, and mutate, in a process remarkably like *mitosis*, the division of cells in a living body. An organization's structure is never static; managers are constantly tweaking it—adding or subtracting layers, changing reporting lines, reorganizing, consolidating. These changes can be small and subtle, as when someone is promoted and not replaced. Or they can be explosive, as when two organizations merge and must consolidate and re-form a host of not-quite-parallel entities.

Whenever the organization structure shifts, communication patterns change, timing is disrupted, power and influence wax and wane, and people get anxious about their own status, security, and general well-being. It's a lot to navigate, and it represents a major source of complexity.

Product and Service Proliferation

Companies naturally want to add to their product and service portfolio so as to get ahead of their competition and delight their customers. But each new product or service makes extra work for R&D, production, sales, and everyone else involved. Even something as simple as changing the label on a product requires marketing input, legal review, graphic design, manufacturing modifications, accounting tracking, warehouse space, sales explanations, and more. And if the old label or product stays on the market, then the variations, all of which need maintenance at some level, proliferate. That is why products and services, even though they are the lifeblood of a company, are major sources of complexity.

Process Evolution

Everything that happens in an organization is accomplished through *processes*, steps for getting work done, many of which cut across levels, departments, and units. The better everyone involved understands these processes and agrees to the steps and their sequence and timing, the faster and more efficiently work flows through the organization. Every time anyone implements an idea about how to do something differently, however, the process flow changes. Even when (as they usually do) these new ideas aim to do the work better or faster, they are likely to affect other people in the chain.

Without careful alignment and general agreement, seeming improvements can backfire. No matter how much discipline is applied, however, new processes are always evolving in an organization—which creates complexity.

Managerial Behavior

As if structural mitosis, product proliferation, and process evolution weren't enough, individual choices and actions also add complexity. Managers provide the day-to-day instructions for people in an organization, reinforcing the basic process flows, overriding or modifying them in the face of changing conditions, or issuing new instructions when processes are missing, unclear, or ambiguous. If the work is routine and repetitive, managers rarely need to deviate from standards. They and their people know what to do, even when someone runs into a problem. That keeps things simple for both managers and employees.

But in dynamic environments, when behaviors and decisions are more fluid, managers have significant latitude for creating work—and thus for making things more complex. They can assign people to do research, collect data, convey information, serve on teams, solve problems, and even develop changes to standard processes. When managers are careful with their instructions, the added complexity can be relatively minor. For example, if a manager puts specific parameters around a new team assignment, clarifies the goal, establishes a time table, and adjusts the team members' regular workload, the complexity level barely changes. However, with a nebulous assignment, an open-ended deadline, and no relief from other tasks, the team members are left to cope as best they can. They will structure their work on the fly, almost certainly without taking the time to consult with others in the process chain, and some tasks may get dropped entirely. The people around the team have to find ways to cope with the changes and lapses, creating additional complexity for everyone.

Unfortunately, many managers unintentionally complexify work by failing to consider the consequences and impact of their instructions.

Making Simplicity into Strategy

Organizations, as social systems with many moving parts, will always be complex—and the dynamic, changing environment will make them even more so. Nonetheless, extreme complexity—complexity that interferes with work and makes it hard for customers to get products and services—is not inevitable. You can stem the tide once you understand the sources of the problem and make a sustained commitment to reducing clutter. But cutting through that clutter takes an ongoing, renewable strategy, not just a simplification shotgun.

There's an old joke about the CEO who attended a presentation about culture change and then turned to his head of HR and said, "Get us one of those." Silly as that sounds, a large number of companies approach many of their major improvements in the same way—the companies focus on employing a tool or an approach that happens to be in fashion rather than developing a broad strategy as part of a business imperative for change.[3]

But real improvement is rarely a one-shot, one-tool endeavor, and reducing complexity is no exception. The ready-made solutions never quite match the real demands of the situation. Several years ago, consultant Bill Jensen conducted a survey of 2,500 people in 460 organizations, finding that most people were suffering from what he called "cognitive overload": too many choices and too little direction. With business information doubling or tripling every few years, he predicted this problem would undoubtedly just get worse.[4]

And it's true. These days, almost every business is struggling with complexity to some degree—and seeing the consequences in terms of employee burnout and turnover, excessive costs and delays, inability to meet customers' expectations, frustration, and exhaustion—despite heavy investments in enterprise information systems, reengineering, balanced scorecards, Six Sigma, and a host of other tools. The problem is that these tools have been applied to particular aspects of complexity—not incorporated in comprehensive strategies and focused on achieving specific business results.

To succeed at simplification and to sustain it over time, you need to understand and address the four main ways that complexity builds up in any human organization—and then create an attack that is tailored to your situation. Table 1-1 lays out the tools and approaches that may be the most appropriate for combating each source of complexity and essentially gives you the building blocks for crafting your own simplification strategy. The structure of the book corresponds to this road map: each of the next four chapters

TABLE 1-1

Road map for simplicity

	Causes of complexity	Approaches for increasing simplicity
Structural mitosis	• Focusing on structure before strategy • Designing based on people and personalities • Building mechanical rather than organic organizations	• Differentiate between core and context • Take a customer perspective • Consolidate similar functions and tasks • Prune layers, and increase spans of control
Product proliferation	• Volume complexity • Support complexity • System complexity • Design complexity	• Portfolio analysis • SKU rationalization and reduction • Customer design partnering
Process evolution	• Local differences • Multiplication of steps and loops • Informality of process • Lack of cross-functional or cross-unit transparency	• Best-practice identification • Process mapping and redesign • Six Sigma and Lean • Rapid results • Work-Out
Managerial behavior	• Overdoing strengths • Avoiding areas of discomfort	• *Strategy, planning, and budgeting:* Decide how much detail is enough • *Goal setting and demand making:* Improve calibration, and avoid the seven deadly sins • *Communications:* Clarify message and who needs to receive it

address one of the four main sources of complexity—first by exploring the unintentional and often unconscious ways that managers create complexity for themselves—and then by describing the tools and approaches that can be used to fight the good fight. As mentioned in the preface, many of these tools are well known, and descriptions with more detail are available elsewhere. The intent of this book, however, is to help you apply these tools strategically to combat complexity over time. The last two chapters of the book illustrate how this can be done—whether you are trying to tackle the entire organization (chapter 6) or just your piece of it (chapter 7).

Countering Complexity at ConAgra Foods

But what does a "simplicity strategy" actually look like in practice? Let's look at the case of ConAgra Foods.

Picture a multibillion-dollar company with more than a hundred consumer brands and no common method for reporting, tracking, or analyzing results. How would you make decisions about relative brand performance? And how would you produce consolidated numbers for investors and analysts? That was what Gary Rodkin faced when he left PepsiCo, Inc., and became CEO of ConAgra Foods in October 2005.

ConAgra's complexity certainly was not planned; it was the byproduct of a growth strategy that had hit the wall. Starting in the 1970s, ConAgra (then a century-old grain milling company) began buying food companies with well-known brands. Since each company had its own niche, ConAgra chose to maintain them as relatively autonomous, independent operations. This strategy fueled tremendous growth, driving ConAgra from revenues of $400 million to a peak of $25 billion in the 1990s; revenues eventually settled at $14 billion after a series of divestitures.

By the time Rodkin arrived at ConAgra, the strategy of maintaining dozens of independent operating companies was clearly no longer viable. Customers were demanding a single face from ConAgra rather than a disconnected series of brand managers, customer service representatives, and shipping clerks. Employees were increasingly frustrated by the competition between operating units, the lack of career paths between units, and the complex and often invisible ways that decisions were made. Analysts were looking for clear, concise, and reliable numbers that would let them track performance of the company as a whole, not just the individual pieces. And investors wanted less of their capital devoted to duplicate functions and more to investments in the most promising brands.

But meeting these demands was not easy, given the fragmented systems, data, processes, and organization. In essence, as Rodkin realized, reducing complexity was not just something nice to do; it was a real business imperative that could make or break the company. Therefore, within thirty days of his arrival, he made simplicity a key element of his public vision for the company and his day-to-day choices as CEO.

Simple Does Not Mean Easy

With this imperative in mind, Rodkin began to attack ConAgra's complexity by focusing first on the company's structure. The starting point was to shift ConAgra from a holding company with multiple units to an integrated operating company. Instead of each brand or collection of brands doing everything for itself, common functions, including product supply, sales, finance, human resources, information technology, R&D, and legal, were combined into enterprise units. The brands were then pulled together into portfolio "operating groups" (snacks, refrigerated, grocery, frozen, and commercial). These operating groups would be accountable for the profitability of the brands—while drawing services from the enterprise functions. The enterprise functions would be account-able for reducing costs and supporting the brands' profit and losses. This structure was put in place before the end of 2005, only a few months after Rodkin's arrival.

While Rodkin was simplifying the organizational structure of the company, a parallel project was under way to simplify the brand structure. In the old ConAgra, all hundred-plus brands had equal status. They competed with one another for marketing and invest-ment dollars—which made planning and resource allocation com-plex free-for-alls. To simplify and rationalize these decisions, by early 2006 the company had sorted the brands into three cate-gories: *growth* (brands to be built up), *manage for cash* (brands to be maintained), and *potential divestment* (brands to be sold). Brands from the last group, including meat brands Armour, Eck-rich, and Butterball Turkey, were immediately put up for sale—and sold later in the year.

The new enterprise functions and brand groups were hardly a cure-all for ConAgra's woes, however, because the processes for running the company were all still geared to the old structure and ways of doing business. For example, sales reports contained hun-dreds of pages of data, but the finance function could not compare and contrast brand results easily, because each brand used its own unit of sale—weights, pallets, cartons, dollars, shipments, cans, whatever had made sense to the brand's original owners. Similarly, the supply chain organization had to provide cans in dozens of sizes, requiring different purchasing procedures, vendors, and manufac-turing processes. Even ingredients were overly complex: as just one example, ConAgra products called for a dozen types of carrots.

What became clear was that simplifying ConAgra's structure and product typology had uncovered a hornet's nest of process complexity. But addressing that was much harder than reorganiz-ing the company or sorting the brands. Each of the myriad ways people had devised for getting things done within and across units had to be examined and rewired (or eliminated or re-created) one at a time. Moreover, much of this had to be done at the enterprise level, which meant that people who had never worked together before (many of whom were used to competing with each other) now had to collaborate. And they had to do all this while keeping the business running.

This was the point at which Rodkin and his senior team realized that the process-simplification effort had to be combined with a conscious focus on changing the culture—so that simplicity would be valued and reinforced as an integral part of the way things were done, along with personal responsibility and willingness to work together. This reaffirmed the mantra of "simplicity, accountability, and collaboration" that Rodkin had established as the operating principles for the new ConAgra when he first arrived.

Engaging in Simplicity

With this underpinning, Rodkin introduced a program he called RoadMap, based on GE's famous Work-Out, which brought together people from across the company to rewire and re-create critical processes—while also making the message of "simplicity, accountability, and collaboration" come alive. An early RoadMap session, for example, focused on simplifying the financial reporting hierarchies so that everyone would report consistent units of measure (pounds or kilograms), product units (cans or cartons), and organization (by division, by brand, by subbrand, and so forth). Representatives of the brand operating groups and the enterprise functions—more than sixty people in all—debated these issues over the course of two days with one simple ground rule: at the end of the two days, they would come to a single decision that they would all recognize and implement. And if they couldn't come to that decision, then the CFO or CEO would decide and they would abide by *that*, regardless of their original preference. As it turned out, the group did come to a decision—which allowed finance and information technology to spend the next several months building a truly company-wide reporting system that was successfully launched in October 2006— exactly one year after Rodkin joined ConAgra.

Throughout 2006, ConAgra held dozens of such RoadMap sessions, entirely rewiring the company's process infrastructure at the enterprise level. To coordinate all these efforts—and to help build the culture of simplicity, accountability, and collaboration— transformation leaders were appointed for each business unit and enterprise function. The transformation leaders worked with their business or function executives to identify and prioritize RoadMap opportunities—processes that needed to be rewired— and to design sessions so that the right people were engaged. The leaders also became a community of change leaders who drove the use of common materials, facilitator training for the sessions, tracking mechanisms, and an overall governance structure to keep the process-simplification efforts on track.

By the end of 2006, ConAgra had a far simpler set of enterprise-wide processes in place for reporting, planning, capital expenditures, new product development and introduction, performance management, and more. In addition, substantial cost savings were already in hand. For example, the Human Resources Business Center (the shared service for HR transactions) managed to handle double the volume without hiring anyone to help, and the Canadian Division reduced inventory write-offs by $1.5 million. Equally important, by this point more than a thousand ConAgra employees had been engaged in simplification efforts—either in RoadMap sessions or on implementation teams—and the culture of simplicity, accountability, and collaboration was starting to take hold.

Developing and leading a simplification strategy for an organization, however, needs to be more than an organizational, analytical, or process-improvement exercise. It also needs to be personal. If you are serious about driving simplification, then you need to identify your own behavior patterns. Chances are, like most managers, you're creating complexity without realizing it, because *all* styles of management can and do cause complexity; they just do it in different ways. Moreover, you cannot expect subordinates to take simplification seriously unless you model commitment to it yourself. Unless you think about your own patterns and ways to shift them toward simplicity, you may discover later that you unconsciously sabotaged the effort.

As part of the overall change effort at ConAgra Foods, Gary Rodkin and each of his senior executives worked with a leadership consultant, both individually and collectively. One element of feedback for Rodkin was that he sometimes failed to specify who should take the lead on a cross-functional or cross-business-unit issue, and the resulting guesswork was leading to what they called "jump balls": multiple executives either assuming that they had the lead or thinking that someone else did—creating confusion, competition, and occasional neglect. By discussing this tendency, Rodkin and his direct reports were able to cut back on jump balls and simplify the resolution of critical issues. In the process, they also realized that this pattern had been replicated in some of the next-level management teams and was creating complexity there. So working it as a collective issue had a powerful impact far beyond Rodkin's own behavior.

Are You Ready for Simplification?

Not everyone is in a position to simplify an entire organization; nor do most organizations require the kind of comprehensive and dramatic strategy that Gary Rodkin launched at ConAgra Foods. Nonetheless, all managers have opportunities to improve results through simplification at their own levels. The question is whether you actually see these opportunities, or whether they have become so routine and ingrained that you no longer even realize they are there. And if you do see them, then the question is whether you want to accept these complexities as regular, day-to-day annoyances or actually do something about them. See "Getting Started" for an easy way of assessing your need to simplify your organization.

Individual decisions like these can mask a huge backlog of potential improvement. At a meeting of the top 120 managers of a large European company, the new CEO asked everyone to brainstorm opportunities for simplification in the four key areas: structure, product, process, and behavior. Within twenty minutes, the group came up with hundreds of ideas: upgrade and simplify the complex job-grading system and make it more consistent across the corporation, create shared services to support multiple businesses in the regions, clarify decision rules (both between corporate and the business units and between levels within units), consolidate reporting units and reduce the number of legal entities, and many others. The funny thing is that every one of these ideas had existed prior to this meeting. Not a single one was new, and in fact many had been bouncing around for years. But until a new CEO came on board and made simplification a priority, everyone had accepted the way things were done in this corporation.

That acceptance of the complexity status quo is a common situation. We all make accommodations and accept suboptimal ways of working with our people and with our customers and partners. We grow numb to complexity—and only begin to address it when customers, costs, or other crises force us into action. But it doesn't have to be this way. Simplification can be an ongoing strategy for your unit or for your company. It can be a way of differentiating you from the competition, strengthening the loyalty and engagement of your employees, and improving your overall organizational effectiveness. And you don't have to wait.

What are the major sources of complexity in your organization?

As a way of getting started, fill out the following questionnaire. Ask your direct reports to fill it out as well—and then enlist others in your organization to participate. Once you have a representative sample, review the answers with your colleagues. The dialogue is what matters here, more than the scores. Use the discussion to raise awareness about complexity and to get people to identify opportunities for simplification that already exist. If you see obvious things you can do right away, feel free to get started. If the opportunities are not directly actionable, then consider this the first step toward building a simplification strategy. The remainder of this book is designed to walk you through the rest.

Instructions: For each question, select answer 1, 2, or 3. Then add up the numbers for each of the four sections and for the overall questionnaire. The maximum score for any section is 15 (five questions—each answered with a 3).

Organization

A. How easily can you draw a picture of your structure—showing major business units, functions, and geographies?

It's simple and straightforward.	1
It takes a little explanation.	2
I would need a computer-aided-design program.	3

B. How many organizational layers are there between the CEO and first-line workers?

Seven or fewer.	1
Eight to ten.	2
More than ten.	3

C. To what extent are similar or duplicate functions across your organization streamlined and consolidated into centers of excellence or shared services?

We actively look for these opportunities.	1
We do this every once in a while.	2
This would be unusual for us.	3

Organization (*continued*)

D. If you had the opportunity to reorganize the company (or your part of it) and you wanted to maintain or improve productivity, what is the minimum percentage of the workforce you would have to keep?

100 percent of our current workforce.	1
About 85 percent of our current workforce.	2
75 percent or less of our current workforce.	3

E. On average, how many people report directly to managers at your company?

Ten or more.	1
Five to nine.	2
Less than five.	3

Total organization _____

Products or services

F. How often do you do a thorough review of your product or service portfolio?

It's a regular practice—once a year or more often.	1
Every couple of years.	2
Can't remember the last time we did this.	3

G. To what extent do you design products or services with simplicity in mind—from both an internal and a customer perspective?

Customers and internal functions actively drive simplification.	1
It's a consideration in our designs.	2
It's an afterthought at best.	3

H. If you could streamline your product or service
lines without reducing profitability, what percentage
would you eliminate?

Just a few.	1
About 15 percent.	2
About 25 percent, or more.	3

I. How many products or services does your
company offer?

A manageable number.	1
A few more than we need.	2
More than we can manage.	3

J. To what extent are your old products or services
phased out when new ones are introduced?

As often as necessary; we have a formalized process.	1
Periodically, but there is no formalized process.	2
Rarely.	3

Total products or services   _____

Process

K. How long does it take for your finance department to
close the books at the end of each reporting period?

Less than one week.	1
One to three weeks.	2
Three weeks or more.	3

L. How many months does it take to create the
budget for the next fiscal year?

Less than two months.	1
Two to four months.	2
Five months or more.	3

Process (*continued*)

M. When you need approval for a capital expense
   or policy modification, how clear are you about
   how to get it?

   I know exactly how to get approval.   1

   I have a reasonable idea of what to do.   2

   I'm not really sure how to go about it.   3

N. How quickly are disputes between functions
   or with customers resolved?

   Right away.   1

   Within a week.   2

   It seems to drag on forever.   3

O. How large a gap exists between your current
   productivity and the productivity targets in your
   strategic goals?

   None.   1

   Some.   2

   A great deal.   3

Total process   _____

Managerial behavior

P. How many employees can accurately describe
   your overall strategic goals?

   Nearly everyone.   1

   About half.   2

   A few.   3

Q. How much time do senior managers spend
   in meetings?

   Less than a quarter of their time.   1

   About half their time.   2

   Most of their time.   3

R. How many people do potential new senior hires need to meet before a hiring decision is made?

Just a few.	1
Four to eight.	2
Nine or more.	3

S. How many of the reports that you produce or read add real value?

Most (roughly 80–100 percent).	1
More than half (50–80 percent).	2
Less than half.	3

T. Approximately how much of your company's internal e-mail adds limited or no value?

Not much (less than 10 percent).	1
Quite a bit (10–30 percent).	2
Too much (over 30 percent).	3

Total managerial behavior _____

Overall total _____

Scoring: *A score of 5 or less in any category suggests that complexity is under control in that area. A score of 6 to 10 is a caution flag; complexity may be creeping upward, and the area should receive increased scrutiny. Over 10 in any one category indicates that complexity may already be out of control and that this should be a focus of your simplification strategy. Overall, a score under 20 is "excellence in simplification." From 21 to 40 is "creeping complexity." Over 40 is "cause for concern."*

Simplifying Structure

O NE OF THE GREAT IRONIES of modern society is that today's complicated organizations were created to simplify complex work. Henry Ford, Frederick Taylor, and other pioneers of the scientific management revolution in the early twentieth century realized that the best way to get things done on a large scale was to break work down into discrete and simple tasks supported by technology. Workers could be organized into units where they would use technology as an aid to doing one or two things well, and do them over and over again, without having to think about how everything fit together. The job of the engineer was to design the tasks, and the job of the manager was to make sure that these tasks were done properly (the right specs, time frame, and cost) and then pass the results on to the next department for further processing or aggregation. It was logical, straightforward, and simple.

This basic paradigm of breaking work into discrete tasks and organizational units and then reaggregating it through managerial direction and controls has been the cornerstone of organizational life ever since. The system's real origins, of course, stretch back much further. One could even argue that it has been part of human organizations from the time of the pharaohs in Egypt or the construction of the Great Wall of China. But when this hierarchical system was coupled with industrial-age technological advances, it produced enormous leaps in productivity, efficiency, and output— essentially fueling the unprecedented standard-of-living advances experienced in many parts of the world.

But in reality, the hierarchical organization design was never as simple as its supporters claimed it to be.

Flaws in Hierarchical Simplicity

To start with, many people do not want to do the same task over and over again, finding it boring or demeaning. Instead, they want to think, to contribute to the bigger picture, to understand how their work makes a difference, and to learn new skills. They also don't want to be told what to do, as though they have no choice. That makes for an inherent tension between workers and managers in a hierarchical organization—between the people doing discrete tasks and the ones who need to make sure that those tasks are done uniformly, without independent thought. Except for people who voluntarily give away their free will to a religious or military order (or are conscripted or coerced into one and become reconciled to their fate), this tension almost always exists.

Even during the early days of the assembly line and the emergence of the hierarchical corporation, there was intense debate about making work too simple and repetitive. Holbrook Fitz John Porter, an early industrial engineer, called for greater "industrial democracy" in the *New York Times* in 1919 and summarized the tension this way:

Half a century ago, industrial establishments were smaller
than they are now, and the employer knew all his men and
their families. He sympathized with them and helped them.
The men appreciated his thoughtfulness for their welfare and
reciprocated in loyalty to his interest. But as time went on and
the size of industrial establishments grew, the business end of
the enterprise engrossed so much of the employer's time that
he had to employ a superintendent to attend to the shop, and
the close touch the employer had with his men was lost to a
large extent. Then came the division of the shop into departments . . . Thus in the gradual expansion of the industrial plant
there occurred a cleavage. The interests of the employer and
employee were no longer mutual; on the contrary, they had
become antagonistic.

To counter this cleavage, Porter proposed a system in which "the
men are encouraged to make suggestions for the betterment of the
plant."[1]

While this debate raged, industrialists continued to refine the
hierarchical model and produce an unprecedented flow of goods.
But the debate about whether this was the right model never really
went away—it just moved from theory to the streets. Labor unions
emerged as alternative power bases to counter managerial control,
formalizing the divide between managers and workers. So right
from the start, the organizational model was complicated with additional managerial controls to keep workers in check, with an alternative power structure (the unions) that pushed back against the
managerial controls, and with additional functions such as labor
lawyers and personnel specialists who were needed to keep the
system in balance.

Furthermore, these early industrial pioneers also learned that
making work simple didn't mean making the organization design

simple. Building big "things"—automobiles, steel bars, railway cars—took many steps. Each step required a different unit or department. And each step needed support functions—engineering, procurement of materials, financial control, hiring and training of workers, selling to customers, and more. So the early organization charts proliferated with multiple departments and sections and then sprouted multiple levels of managers to organize and control them.

As technology and education advanced, more and more variations were introduced into these basic organization designs. Product design engineers were joined by engineers for metallurgy, for machine tools, and for other specialties, each of which needed its own department. Similarly, rather than generalists in finance, the firms needed controllers, analysts, tax specialists, financial planners, and so on.

And then the consumers introduced yet more complexity. Henry Ford's idea was to build one type of car, with standard materials, in one color. That made things relatively simple. But people wanted different types and models of cars, with different colors and features. The black Model T alone was not enough. This made organization structures proliferate and expand even further. By the end of World War II, the Western world had created not only incredibly productive industrial machines but incredibly complex organizations, with dozens of units, functions, departments, product groups, brands, levels, layers, titles, and more.

So what started out as a simple way to produce goods and services on a large scale quickly became the extremely complex organizational system that we know today. I describe the condition as "structural mitosis" because organizations are constantly being divided and redivided into new units and departments—just as cells divide and redivide into more complex and not always benign biological structures.

Three Unwitting Complexity Traps
in Designing Organizations

Organizational structures, of course, do not just emerge like Athena from the brow of Zeus. Managers design organizational structures according to their best judgment about how to break out tasks, assign work, and control the overall enterprise, and then they foster structural mitosis as they continue to tweak and redesign these structures. Three common traps lie in wait for managers as they create these designs:

- Focusing on structure before strategy

- Designing according to people and personalities

- Building mechanical rather than organic organizations

Structure Before Strategy

From earliest childhood and throughout life, most people want to know where they fit in—with their family, school, community, social network, work organization. So it is no wonder that managers spend so much time refining an organization's design in an effort to make sure that people always know who they report to and what they are supposed to do—before knowing exactly what the design is supposed to accomplish.

A number of years ago, my colleagues and I worked with a copier company that was struggling to survive in the face of very tough competition both from U.S. and Japanese rivals. The one thing that this company had going for it was a proprietary toner technology that allowed its copiers to run with less heat, and operate at lower cost and with greater reliability, than those of the other major players. If anything was going to save the company, it would be this technology. However, the senior managers, most of whom had come up through the ranks of copier sales, were very uncomfortable dealing with strategic questions about new product development, engineering investments, and applied research.

So instead they focused on how to organize marketing and sales to provide clarity to the vast majority of their colleagues, who were going head-to-head with the other copier companies in the marketplace. R&D became a disconnected distant cousin, almost run as a separate company. But without a strong feedback loop from sales into R&D—and a steady stream of new products and features based on the proprietary technology—the sales and marketing folks were at a competitive disadvantage. To win more business, the senior team kept changing the structure of the branch organization and the national accounts team, setting up new channel structures and making other changes—all of which made life more and more complicated for everyone—and most of which made no difference in sales. Eventually, the company was taken over by a Japanese rival that focused on the technology—and essentially outsourced and simplified marketing and sales.

In retrospect, it's easy to see that the leaders of the copier company should have first agreed on a growth strategy that exploited their technology, and only then designed an organization structure aimed at carrying out that strategy. This would have made the company less complicated and possibly more successful.

In the heat of battle, however, it's not so easy to see the root cause of why things have gotten complicated. Instead, performance issues compel managers to keep making seemingly logical tactical adjustments. While each move makes sense on its own, the combination creates a constant series of mitotic changes that add more and more complexity. For example, at the copier company, the struggle for net sales growth led to a large inventory of equipment that had gone off lease. Sales branches had been responsible for reselling these machines, but as inventory grew, management decided to create a new headquarters department for equipment resale. Sensible enough on paper—but in practice, the new department added new levels of approvals, new procedures, new programs and incentives, new reports, and new staff to manage it all. In the end, the salespeople viewed the equipment resale department as one more unnecessary complication from headquarters that made their jobs that much more difficult. But once created, the department was very difficult to dismantle and in essence took on a life of its own.

Being in a complex organizational structure is like being in the middle of a maze with no map for getting out. It pays to pause and ask whether your strategy for success is clear—and whether your organization structure is aligned with that strategy. Otherwise, tactical changes may just force you and your people to run faster and faster through the maze—without increasing your chances of finding the exit.

People and Personalities

While organizational structures are often portrayed as sets of interconnected boxes, the reality is that the boxes contain human beings with strengths, weaknesses, and personalities. And often these human characteristics don't fit with the logic of the organizational design. As a result, managers will often make accommodations to the design so that the existing people will be comfortable.

A few years ago, I worked with the CEO of a hospital that was trying to tighten operational procedures, reduce costs, and improve patient care. One of the key strategic opportunities was to enlarge the outpatient clinics so that the hospital could use its expert resources to treat more people without adding more beds. To make this happen, it needed much more discipline in the management of the outpatient clinics—standard intake procedures;

routinized billing and collection; agreed-upon protocols for various types of patient services, follow-up procedures, and so on. Unfortunately, the physician in charge of the clinics was not skilled in management and not willing to impose standards on the other clinic doctors. Although the CEO realized that this senior manager was not the right fit for implementing the clinic strategy, he valued her loyalty and ability to work with clinic staff. Rather than replacing her in that role, the CEO brought in a chief operating officer (COO) for the outpatient department, and the COO in turn brought in submanagers for a number of the clinics. Eventually, the overall structure was more complex, with added layers and fuzzy accountability—and the strategic goals were still not achieved.

Almost everyone who has worked in a large organization has seen this pattern—changing the structure to suit the people, rather than getting the right people to run the structure the organization needs. Over time, these kinds of accommodations create inefficiency, confusion, and overall complexity. The classic case was the aftermath of the Travelers-Citibank merger in 1998. Instead of making a clear decision about who would head the combined company, Sandy Weil and John Reed became co-CEOs. This two-headed structure was mirrored in many of the departments, where it was decided to appoint coheads (one from Citibank and one from Travelers) who would work together to run their areas. Of course, each cohead needed staff and support people, so the structures quickly became bloated, complicated, and ineffective—and in many cases, the two coheads competed with each other rather than collaborating.

Citi-Travelers is an extreme case, but the dynamic itself is very common. Rather than lose good people or force them into positions where they might struggle, we often adjust the organization to fit the strengths or comfort levels of the current staff. While this kind of accommodation might feel good in the short run, it almost always makes for confusion and tangles down the road. So again, if you are trapped in a complex organization, pause and ask yourself whether the structure has perhaps been designed around the limitations of its managers.

Mechanical Rather Than Organic Designs

Everyone recognizes the standard organization chart—a series of boxes and interconnected lines meant to portray the way an organization is structured. It has become such an accepted way of thinking about organizations that it's even included in Microsoft's PowerPoint and most other presentation software packages. All you have to do is put names in the boxes, and voilà—you have an organization.

Unfortunately, the box-and-line design is a product of the industrial engineering assumptions of the early twentieth century. The boxes are meant to limit those within them to specific tasks, functions, and roles—and the lines are meant to convey hierarchical relationships. But such a chart doesn't capture the reality: organizations are dynamic, living entities that evolve and change all the time as new people come on board, new products are added, new processes develop, new customers and markets open up, and new environmental conditions emerge. Moreover, most work consists of processes that cut across the boxes horizontally, so a lot of people find it impossible to sit in their boxes and "go through channels" to get what they need for their jobs. The whole idea that an organization is some kind of machine with a static blueprint is basically outmoded.[2]

When managers design company structures, however, they still use the standard hierarchical organization chart, mostly because they don't have tools designed for today's organic organizations. This immediately creates some degree of complexity, because the official chart does not match the way things really work. The deeper trap opens, however, when—in the fond belief that the mechanical design really does reflect organizational reality—people try to fine-tune it to make it more and more perfect. This almost inevitably results in even greater complexity as the formal structure becomes yet more misaligned with actual behavior.

A number of years ago, I worked with Siemens on a leadership program. Many managers said they were finding it difficult to function effectively in the global matrix organization that confronted them. They were in businesses structured into product or technology groups, each of which had to coordinate with geographic organizations for countries and regions. And all of them had to deal with functions (such as finance, HR, and legal) that cut across both products and geographies. Charts described these relationships and who reported to whom—but when they were all put together, the structure was so tangled that few managers could figure it out. The mechanics were in place, but they didn't match what it took to make the business successful.

In contrast, GE Capital, which in the 1990s had dozens of businesses, many of which were global as well, functioned without a traditional organization chart. CEO Gary Wendt organized the company on the basis of a one-page diagram that he called a "bubble chart." In the center of the page were the corporate services provided out of GE Capital's headquarters—finance, human resources, legal, and others. The separate business units were then portrayed as "bubbles" coming out of the center. Each "bubble business" had a president who organized it in a way that would best meet its goals. Whenever a business became too large, unwieldy, and complex, Wendt would divide it into a couple of smaller businesses or combine it with another business that would provide synergy. It was truly an organic organization structure—constantly shifting in accord with business needs. This flexibility and simplicity allowed

GE Capital to be one of the major growth engines for GE during that period.

Again, if you feel trapped in a maze of organizational complexity, a third question that you can ask is whether your design is so mechanical that it robs you of the flexibility to adjust to changing business conditions.

Starting Over: How to Get Out of the Complexity Traps

Imagine that you have just been appointed to a new job that comes with the freedom to design or redesign your organization. How do you create a structure that minimizes complexity? Besides watching out for the three traps, apply these four principles:

- Differentiate between core and context.

- Take a customer perspective.

- Consolidate similar functions and tasks.

- Prune layers, and increase spans of control.

Core Versus Context

Geoffrey Moore, a consultant who works with technology and other rapid-growth companies, suggests a useful distinction he refers to as "core" and "context."[3] *Core* parts of an organization are those functions, units, or activities that drive the business strategy—and therefore should be uniquely owned and self-operated because they provide a competitive advantage. *Context* functions or units support the core areas but are not particularly unique; their services could be bought from others. One way to avoid the structure-before-strategy trap is to take a hard look at the core and context question as part of designing your organization. Concentrate on the core parts of the business first, and then automate, outsource, streamline, or reduce costs for the context activities (as long as this doesn't interfere with core work).

For example, at the copier company that distracted itself by refining its sales operation, an analysis of core activities would have highlighted the critical role of research and product development. The managers might then have created a better link between R&D and the sales teams. Likewise, they might have decided that selling off-lease equipment was a nonessential function with no particular competitive advantage (other than improving the balance sheet). So they might have spun it off as a separate business unit with its own profit and loss statements.

Pitney Bowes did just that with its entire copier business in 2001. Realizing that selling copiers was not part of the Pitney Bowes core—document management and mailing services—CEO Michael Critelli worked with the board to set up Imagistics, a separate company that would focus exclusively on copiers. The Pitney Bowes COO, Marc Breslawsky, became CEO of the new company— and both companies turned out to be successful. What was context for Pitney Bowes (copiers) became core for Imagistics.

Customer Perspective

A second principle for reducing complexity is to design your organization from your customers' perspective. How can you make it as easy as possible for people to do business with you?

I remember learning this lesson from one of my early consulting experiences with what was then Chase Manhattan Bank. At the time, most of the bank was organized into product groups, each selling its offerings independently. The main exception was the Corporate Banking division, which was organized around large clients and which assigned "relationship managers" to them. But these relationship managers focused on corporate lending, ignoring the myriad other products offered by Chase. Because of this structure, the head of Corporate Banking at the time realized that he had no real idea how much business the bank was doing with any customer or what the consolidated risk profile might be. Furthermore, he wondered whether the bank was missing opportunities to do more business with its very best blue-chip clients. As an experiment, we sent out a notice that on a certain day, he was having a meeting for everyone who was doing business with one particular customer. When he arrived at the meeting room, it was standing room only. More than forty units in the bank were doing something with this customer, and most of them were not aware of what the others were doing. Imagine how the customer felt while being besieged by multiple bankers from the same institution!

As a result of this experiment, Chase decided to strengthen the role of the corporate relationship manager, reduce the direct sales capability of product groups, and take a more coordinated approach to key client relationships. Not only did this increase the bank's profitability and help it manage its risk, but the change made it much simpler for customers to do business with Chase. Viewing the organization from the outside in doesn't need to trigger a major restructuring, which might even make things more complicated, but it does help to provide orientation for how different units work with each other more simply.

For example, the enterprise business (large corporate customer business) of Cisco Systems is a classic matrix in which geographically based account executives work with product and service organizations to support their customers. Despite the tensions and complications caused by this matrix structure, it has been in place for many years; people know how to get things done, the accounting and reporting systems are in place, and the account execs provide a point of coordination and accountability. So, for the most part, customers are satisfied with the structure. However, in late 2006, a number of customers began to comment that Cisco's structure did not foster the deep industry expertise that would help them develop solutions to their unique problems, which is what many of them were looking for from their technology partners. Rather than reconfigure the entire organization and create even more complexity, Cisco appointed Patrick Finn to be a new vice president for industry "verticals" and asked him to address the customers' issue without essentially changing the overall structure. What Finn did was to assemble a small team of "domain experts" for each "vertical," such as health care, government, education, financial services, and retail. The teams focused on developing industry expertise that could be used to make the existing account executives smarter about their industries, thus addressing the customers' needs without overly complicating the organization. And oh, by the way, sales improved significantly.

Consolidation

One symptom of structural mitosis is the existence of multiple units doing identical or similar tasks—or the same tasks or functions being done in different places. Sometimes, these can be core functions of the business—as when a company has several different sales forces. At other times, they can be context functions, such as administrative support for sales or financial reporting for different legal entities. In any case, whenever these kinds of redundancies are identified, a third principle for design simplicity is to explore the possibility of consolidating them in one place. Once they are consolidated, it is then easier to automate, outsource, or otherwise improve the cost-effectiveness and quality of these functions.

Most large organizations have moved in this direction in the past decade through the creation of shared services centers and

FIGURE 2-1

Simplification through consolidation

		Volume	
		High	Low
Expertise needed	High	Center of excellence	Outsourced consulting
	Low	Service center	Aggregation

centers of excellence. The simple way to think about this is to use the two-by-two matrix shown in figure 2-1.

One dimension of this matrix is the volume of the activity or function. Is it done frequently across the organization? The other dimension is the degree of unique expertise or company or industry knowledge needed to do this activity effectively. How much expertise does it require?

For activities that are done very frequently and require specialized expertise, the simplification strategy would be to form a *center of excellence* (COE). For example, one of the ways that ConAgra Foods simplified its structure was to create a center of excellence for advertising—a core function for a consumer packaged goods company. Previously, each brand team had developed its own advertising strategy and then worked with agencies to translate the strategy into television, print, or interactive ads. With so many people involved, the overall process was not only costly, but also inconsistent in terms of time and quality. Creating a center of excellence for advertising was a way for ConAgra to have all its ads developed and managed in one place—with a consistent process—and to have the creative development be directed by people who had even higher degrees of expertise and experience. In this new structure, the brand teams were able to focus on their brand strategies, and the advertising COE could take it from there. The result was a significant reduction in the number of people on the brand teams and a dramatically reduced cycle time for getting ads developed and produced.

For high-volume context activities, which do not require specialized industry knowledge, a *service center* is likely to be the way to go. Typical tasks that fall into this category include accounting transactions (payroll processing, payables, receivables, legal-entity reporting), human resources transactions (benefits administration, company and personnel information management), sales and marketing support, information technology technical support, and other types of back-office processing. Consolidating these tasks in service centers allows the large volumes to be managed at agreed-upon service levels most efficiently and simply.

Most companies move toward service centers in an evolutionary way. They first identify the functions or tasks that are being done in different places and that can be consolidated. They assess whether those tasks need to be done at all (asking, "Do we really need this report?" and similar questions), and if so, whether the tasks offer immediate opportunities for simplification and streamlining. Sometimes, these immediate opportunities are quite substantial. For example, when the conglomerate A.P. Moller-Maersk began thinking about how it could simplify its financial reporting, it had to address the proliferation of legal entities that had been created over many years. Consolidating legal entities would eliminate much of the reporting at one stroke. CEO Nils Andersen and CFO Soren Thorup Sorenson then formed cross-functional task forces—and reduced hundreds of board "seats" in the next year.

Once high-volume context activities have been cleaned up, a single manager can take responsibility for bringing them together, doing them the same way, and eventually doing them in the same place at less cost. Over time, this manager can drive further improvement through automation and process redesign. Eventually, if it makes financial sense and quality can be maintained, the entire function or unit is either moved to a less expensive location or outsourced to a company that does this activity for a living, that is, where this activity is core instead of context.

When Patrick O'Sullivan headed the finance function for Zurich Financial Services worldwide, he drove this kind of evolution with most of his area's transactional and back-office activities. Over the course of five years, functions such as tax analysis, financial reporting, and cash management—all of which had been done separately and slightly differently in each of the company's business units—were gradually streamlined, consolidated, and then outsourced to providers in India. This evolution not only drove simplification throughout the company by reducing process variations and multiple locations, but also saved hundreds of millions of dollars for Zurich.

Of course, not all activities have enough volume to warrant consolidation into a separate unit. Something that requires significant technical or company expertise but is not done very frequently is a candidate for *outsourced consulting.* In other words, the low volume does not warrant having a full-time expert on staff, so when the service is needed, the company is better off buying it externally. If the service is core to the business and requires an ongoing knowledge of the company, the external provider can be a preferred partner who develops a relationship and history over time. This kind of arrangement is straightforward and characterizes many of the professional services provided to organizations. It should be examined periodically, however, to see if the volume or need for expertise changes, which might move it into one of the other categories.

The fourth quadrant of the matrix is the most problematic. Noncore tasks that don't require high levels of specialized expertise often show up in many places simultaneously, but without enough volume to warrant a full-time staff in any one place. Many traditional administrative support tasks, such as scheduling meetings and answering phones, fall into this category. Professional tasks such as preparing presentation slides and doing literature reviews might also be included. The challenge with these types of tasks is that they cause people to use their time in fragmented ways with many interruptions, which complicates their day-to-day work. And on an organizational level, the fragmentation means that most of these tasks are not done efficiently. In the past, companies dealt with some of these tasks by creating resource pools, or *aggregations*, of typists or clerks who would share administrative tasks and load-level the work. Essentially, the low-volume work was aggregated in one place so that it could be done with less fragmentation and more efficiency.

With the advent of today's communications technology, this concept of aggregating low-volume, low-expertise tasks can be taken to a whole new level. Pfizer's Jordan Cohen, a pioneer in this area, calls it the "Office of the Future." His notion is to take things that a lot of people do a little bit of and use technology to enable a few people (who happen to be part of an outsourced company) to do them on a full-time basis. Cohen's Office of the Future (OOF) offers five such services to more than ten thousand Pfizer managers (and the number is growing): secondary research, document creation (slides, flip chart typing, digital images), spreadsheet "jockey work" (entering, parsing, and setting up data), meeting support (scheduling appointments, reserving rooms), and project support (repeatable tasks). For each of these services, Cohen and his team make sure that the work is sufficiently structured and repeatable to hand off to a person in a low-cost location. All a Pfizer manager brought the total from 490 to 1080.[5] Over time, the magic number of direct reports—what most studies proposed would provide optimal interaction, attention, and control—was from five to seven. Some studies suggested that at lower levels of the organization, where work is more routine, somewhat larger spans of control were possible.

Of course, the assumption behind the entire span concept is that the job of the manager is to control subordinates—and in the traditional hierarchical organization, that is certainly the case. However, as organizations become more organic, boundaryless, fluid, and dynamic, the job of the manager changes. No longer is the manager's primary function to aggregate pieces of work done by subordinates and control these subordinates' activities; rather, it is to foster teamwork and communication and to provide inspiration and direction. In short, it is more about leadership and adding value than about control.

Once managers stop trying to exert personal control over subordinates and instead focus on adding value, the number of direct reports can increase substantially. GE discovered this in the early 1990s, when it increased spans of control in many of its businesses from the traditional five, six, or seven to upwards of ten. What happened in most cases was that managers were forced to loosen their controls—just as the theories of span of control would have predicted. There wasn't enough time in the day to check up on everybody as in the past. Now, however, the loss of control was an advantage; when they had to allow their subordinates to be more empowered, managers began to focus on how to add value in other ways—through strategy development, increased customer contact, process improvement, and coaching.

If spans of control are increased, the number of hierarchical layers or levels can be reduced. For example, instead of one

needs to do is click on the desktop "OOF" icon to send w
directly to the support team in India or elsewhere, or talk with
of the outsourced team members if the work requires explana
For example, a Pfizer new business director "oofed" (ye
turned into a verb) a research project on the blood-subs
market—a project that would have taken her months. Th
estate division used OOF support to update and then keep
its detailed records of office usage around the world, requiri
dreds of phone calls and data entry tasks. Even the offic
chairman and CEO found the OOF to be a valuable reso
streamlining its work.[4]

So functions, departments, and tasks can be conso
many ways, depending on the activities involved, their i
to the organization, their frequency, and their cost. In ge
ing fewer units or departments—where people can put
on critical core activities and not be distracted by con
makes an organization simpler.

De-layering

The fourth and final principle for creating a simpler
structure is to cut back on the number of hierarchic
usually requires increasing the number of people v
manager, commonly referred to as *span of control.*

The span-of-control concept was developed ear
eth century as managers tried to determine how mu
and attention supervisors could give to their dir
too many direct reports, the theory ran, the sup
be able to provide adequate control. Many s
conducted, including mathematical analyses o
patterns between boss and subordinates. On
example, that going from four to five subordinat
tial interactions from 44 to 100, and that going

manager having five direct reports—each of whom receives reports from three people—the middle layer could be eliminated and the manager would then have fifteen subordinates. Not only does this dramatically reduce costs by having fewer managers, but it also makes it simpler for ideas and information to flow up and down through the organization. With many layers, communication from the top of the organization to the bottom is a real-life game of "telephone"—messages do get distorted and changed as they work their way from person to person. What's worse is that ideas and information don't move upward quickly and easily, either. At each level, well-meaning managers want to massage the data, ask new questions, put their own spin on an idea, or stop something from proceeding upward altogether. Sometimes, this is appropriate—but more often than not, it creates complicated, convoluted, and even constipated communications in an organization.

For example, when Jeff Kindler became CEO of Pfizer in 2006, he found that as many as fourteen layers of management separated him from the frontline troops in various parts of the company, and that these layers were slowing down or stopping critical information and burdening Pfizer with extra costs. In one case, the sales manager for one of Pfizer's largest customers had to report through a district manager, a regional manager, an area manager, a sales operations manager, a senior sales manager, and an executive sales manager to convey what was happening with that customer. Similarly, in R&D, the lifeblood of the company, scientists were reporting up through a dozen layers of management before getting to an executive. To simplify communications and help the company become less costly and more nimble, Kindler and his head of HR, Mary McLeod, required each of the senior managers to de-layer their organizations so that no more than ten layers separated the CEO from the front line, and preferably no more than eight. Martin

Mackay, president of Pfizer's R&D organization, did even better—reducing layers of management between scientists and top executives to seven.[6]

GlaxoSmithKline IT: Simplifying Structure Pays Off

When Ford Calhoun became chief information officer (CIO) of GlaxoSmithKline Pharmaceuticals in 2001, he inherited an organization that was in desperate need of simplification. The company had just undergone a merger (Glaxo Wellcome with SmithKline Beecham), and information technology (IT) had a number of redundant or independent departments around the world. Costs were high, service standards for internal customers were inconsistent, and it generally took way too long to get things done. Moreover, the IT function was not perceived as an enabler, a driver, or a key factor in making the company more competitive and successful; instead, it was viewed as a necessary cost of doing business.

Calhoun took on the challenge of changing all that and making IT into a competitive advantage for GSK—and simplification was a key element of his strategy. His starting point was the design of a single integrated organization structure for the five thousand people in the IT function across the new company. Both premerger companies had suffered greatly from structural mitosis. Some businesses had their own IT departments, and others were getting services from a corporate unit.

The strategic imperative for the new IT organization was to reduce costs and improve basic IT service levels—and Calhoun's intention was to design the structure to align with this strategy. To achieve this, Calhoun created the three-part IT organization sketched in figure 2-2: support units dedicated to the unique needs

FIGURE 2-2

GlaxoSmithKline IT organization

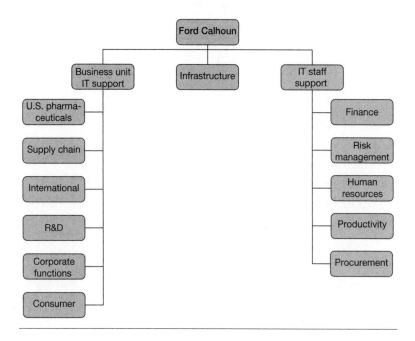

of each business or core function; a corporate infrastructure group for generic computing needs that respond to scale and standardization; and a number of staff functions. All twelve of these areas reported to Calhoun directly, although the dedicated IT support units also reported on a dotted-line basis to their business clients. (Note that the figure, being generated by organizational chart software, is incapable of reflecting the true structure. Of the three boxes in the second row, only the middle one has an officer sitting in it. The other two simply define categories of units that all reported straight to Calhoun.)

Simultaneous with crystallizing the high-level structure was the appointment of people to lead the various units so that the function would not fall into the accommodation trap over time. Rigorous criteria were used for selection, along with an attempt to get a mix of Glaxo Wellcome and SmithKline Beecham people and a diverse management team. Not all the resulting decisions proved correct, but expectations were created that performance would be the ultimate driver, so some sorting out of managers at the first couple of levels continued for a year as it became clear who could step up and who was struggling.

Another element of the new, simplified IT organization was the conscious reduction of layers. Calhoun believed that additional layers not only added costs, but also obscured accountability—making it more complicated to get things done. Calhoun therefore designed the organization so that he would have twelve direct reports with clear and focused accountability, and he expected his managers to have similarly wide spans of control and no more than four layers beneath them. To drive this concept with discipline, Calhoun created an instrument called the Lindex (layers index) and reviewed it with his managers every quarter.

The origin of the Lindex was an article Calhoun had read about the organization structure of the Canadian civil service.[7] Calhoun adapted this article's formula for assessing functional health (based on the average length of communication chains from the top to the bottom of a hierarchy) so that his managers could compute their own Lindex scores. This gave Calhoun a quick snapshot of the organizations, which his managers had to be prepared to discuss. At first, the resulting sessions were somewhat difficult and uncomfortable—but eventually, the managers learned how to use the Lindex, and the logic behind it, to manage the inevitable evolutions in their organizations without adding unnecessary layers.

The simpler organization structure that Calhoun created for GSK allowed him to achieve and sustain substantial cost savings. By 2003, two years after the merger, the IT function had reduced its fixed costs by over $100 million and had six hundred fewer people. More important, this smaller and more streamlined organization was delivering far more services at a far higher level. At the time of the merger in 2001, project cycle times for business application projects—from approval to delivery of benefits—averaged more than one hundred weeks and many projects failed to deliver measurable business benefits at all. By 2003, cycle times were down to an average of twenty-nine weeks and the calculated return on investment in IT projects had doubled. In addition, Calhoun and his team had launched a number of new strategic programs in areas of infrastructure service, Web enablement, enterprise resource planning, and collaboration tools.

Over the next several years, Calhoun maintained the same basic structure but continued to look for opportunities to simplify it and increase the business benefits even further. For example, one of the decentralized IT activities was applications maintenance. Since organizations tend to have thousands of business applications, all of which have different versions, this activity can be very costly and can touch many people—users, developers, data center managers who need to run the applications, finance people who manage licenses for software, help desk staff who work on application-related problems, risk managers who develop contingencies in case an application fails, and others. Rather than continue this fragmented approach, Calhoun began evolving an applications service center within the infrastructure organization, with the charge of simplifying the process and reducing the costs. The manager of this unit inventoried major applications and began eliminating redundant or otherwise unnecessary ones. He developed standards for new applications to make sure they would be compatible with the infrastructure, and he also developed processes for managing applications more effectively. This resulted in further cost reductions—and fewer problems with applications in general.

In addition to creating new units to consolidate and streamline activities, Calhoun looked for opportunities to shed units or move them to lower-cost locations. This led to offshoring or outsourcing of functions such as help desks, applications development, and others. By the end of 2006—five years after the merger between Glaxo Wellcome and SmithKline Beecham—the IT function was contributing $1 billion annually in operating efficiency to the new company.

You Can Design for Simplicity

As the GSK example illustrates, countering structural mitosis is not a one-shot deal—it's an ongoing, iterative process. Competitive conditions change, new technologies and opportunities emerge, people come and go, and organizations are constantly in some degree of flux. To drive simplicity, managers therefore need to keep asking themselves about the three traps of complexity raised in this chapter: *To what extent is our structure aligned with our strategy? To what extent do our managers' skills match the structure that we've created? To what extent is our structure sufficiently organic and flexible to adapt as needed?*

If your answers to these questions move into negative territory, then you may need to revisit the guidelines for making the structure as simple as possible:

- Differentiate between core and context.

- Take a customer perspective.

- Consolidate similar functions and tasks.

- Prune layers, and increase spans of control.

None of this is easy work, and nobody wants to constantly reorganize and create disruptions, potentially fostering even more complexity. However, keeping the organization static while the world around it changes is usually a prescription for failure. In the long run, you'll be better off making periodic shifts rather than waiting for complexity to paralyze your organization and force you to turn everything upside down.

THREE

Reducing Product Proliferation

WHAT IF YOUR PRODUCTS WERE inhibiting your growth instead of driving it? That's what Paul van de Geijn faced when he took over the global life insurance business of Zurich Financial Service in 2003. At the time, Zurich's life insurance business generated $20 billion in gross written premiums and was a key business line around the world. However, the growth rate was only about 1 percent and the industry was becoming more and more crowded with competitors. Moreover, Zurich's sales were mostly through distributors (agents), many of whom also sold other companies' products. So unless Zurich Global Life Insurance's products were more attractive than the competitors', the distributors would not give Zurich priority, which would reduce the growth rate even further.

As Van de Geijn and his team looked for ways to stimulate growth, they realized that one of the keys to success was making it easier to do business with Zurich—both for consumers and for distributors. Since the industry as a whole did not do this well, it represented an opportunity to truly outperform the competition. Historically, Zurich, like most other insurance companies, focused on adding new products or new bells and whistles to old products, and then turned over the new and modified products to underwriters and risk managers, who were supposed to make sure that only the right customers bought the products. As a result, the products themselves became more and more complex and difficult for distributors to explain. In addition, the application and qualification process became extremely rigorous and time-consuming—and thus screened out not only the wrong customers but many potential good customers as well.

So it was tough for customers and distributors to do business with Zurich and getting tougher. A team led by Christian Merk discovered examples like these:

- The benefits of life insurance were explained in complex brochures that also elaborated on financial product benefits and technical features that neither the consumers nor the distributors could easily understand.

- Applications for life insurance required customers to provide the same information more than once, such as giving both age and (two questions further) date of birth.

- In Italy, distributors had to use eighteen different application forms and were required to ask for eight signatures from each customer.

- When policies expired, customers received impersonal, technical letters without concrete suggestions or advice about how to renew their coverage or reinvest their money. More significantly, nobody called the customers in advance to alert them that their policies were about to expire.

- When customers canceled their policies, no one asked for any details or explanations, or offered any alternatives. Instead, the cancellation (and the lost customer) was simply accepted and processed—and the customer was forgotten.

- The application process itself took up to six weeks, and a large number of potential customers decided to call a halt halfway through.

- The huge so-called lead lists sent to distributors were assembled without reference to qualification criteria. As a result, in most countries it was taking at least a hundred customer calls to sell one extra product.

Looking at these and similar insights, Van de Geijn and his team developed a concerted simplification effort that came to be known as "Make Life EaZy" (with a capital Z for Zurich), led by Christian Merk. The effort was launched at an international workshop in Barcelona for Zurich Global Life's top operational managers from fifteen European countries, and as a kickoff exercise, they were given five minutes to fill in their own country's application form for the simplest type of life insurance. When nobody could complete the form in the allotted time, Van de Geijn's managers began to realize that they had a major opportunity—and challenge—on their hands.

To meet the challenge, Merk pulled together a team of Make Life EaZy consultants who flew from country to country to facilitate simplification projects, report best practices, and measure progress.[1] Their job also was to identify and train local staff members as "EaZy Challengers" who would then engage customers, distributors, and employees in their country to identify opportunities to simplify products and services (to make the "Life" business "eaZier"). If ideas were applicable only to that country, they were implemented there; if they applied more broadly to entire product lines or service offerings, they were brought to a head office team for consideration and possible implementation across countries and eventually placed in a shared best-practices database and leveraged across Europe. In the first year, eight countries participated, with more countries added in subsequent years. The effort produced changes such as these:

- *Easier for distributors to sell:* Sales increased by 7 percent after real-life customer stories replaced technical, product-oriented brochures. In these stories, customers tell why they needed life insurance and their satisfaction with their choices. In addition, distributors were provided with videos and other eye-catching, easy-to-understand materials to make sales easier.

- *Easier for customers to reinvest:* The reinvestment rate (buying new products when old ones mature) increased from 14 percent to 38 percent when the impersonal renewal letters were discarded. Instead, Zurich created new letters in simpler language showing the results of the original product and suggesting a number of reinvestment opportunities.

- *Easier to apply for insurance:* The number of application forms in European countries was reduced from eighteen to four by combining application forms based on responsible regulators. At the same time, the number of signatures required on these forms was reduced from eight to three, and 50 percent of the questions were eliminated.

- *Easier to retain customers:* In Germany, the retention rate of customers about to cancel their policies increased from

2 percent to 33 percent after Zurich created a dedicated telephone sales desk to talk with customers whose policies were expiring. The salespeople were trained in understanding the common reasons for cancelling insurance and how to discuss alternatives that could be helpful to customers.

Five years after Make Life EaZy began, the growth rate for Zurich's European life insurance business was at 7 percent, and the new head of the global life business, Mario Greco, was making the program an ongoing part of his management process worldwide.

How Products and Services Unwittingly Contribute to Complexity

As the Zurich Global Life case illustrates, product and service complexity can creep into an organization in a number of ways—including the volume of products, their design, and the way they are sold and serviced. Generally this kind of complexity develops over time as managers seek to win and retain customers and differentiate themselves from their competition by changing the nature of their products—which is exactly what business leaders are supposed to do. At some point, however, the accumulation of these product-related changes either becomes so confusing or adds so much to the total cost of production that it becomes a competitive disadvantage. For example, adding more features to Zurich's basic life insurance product led to changes in the application form, the underwriting process, the brochures, and the servicing of the policy over time—and also made it more difficult both for distributors to explain the product and for customers to understand it. While each change by itself was the right thing to do competitively, the overuse of "doing the right thing" eventually created so much complexity that the company began to sink under its own weight.

This dynamic is present not only in for-profit enterprises but also with nonprofits and public sector organizations. Governments create agencies and then give them additional mandates, missions, regulations, and rules for how the agencies provide services, all of which are interpreted by people who are either trying to add value (in the best cases) or trying to justify their jobs (in the worst cases). Whatever the motivation, the result eventually is a proliferation of services and accompanying procedures that make little sense to citizens and are costly and bureaucratic to provide. For example, during the Clinton administration, Vice President Al Gore led an effort called "reinventing government," which focused on streamlining services at the federal level and resulted in billions of dollars of budget savings. Similar efforts took place in many state governments and in multilateral agencies such as the United Nations and the World Bank. But unless these initiatives are continually renewed and reinvigorated, the normal forces of product and service proliferation continue to add cost and complexity, which is why government or agency simplification remains an issue in almost every election or appointment to office.

Product or service complexity usually has one or more of these four causes:

- *Volume complexity:* Adding to the number of products or services offered, and adding features to existing products or services.

- *Support complexity:* Giving customers unclear instructions on how to use products and get help when needed.

- *System complexity:* Failing to integrate products and services with offerings from other companies in the context of the customer's business.

- *Design complexity:* Building too many bells and whistles into new product and service offerings—without the customer's perspective in mind.

Volume Complexity: Too Much of a Good Thing

Everyone knows the problems that arise when young children go to a candy store: everything looks so good that they are tempted to buy too much, which gets them sick or wastes their parents' money, or both. Being selective and just choosing one or two treats is far easier said than done at any age, and managing your organization's product portfolio entails much the same challenge. It is difficult to be selective and to choose between alternatives that all look good. As a result, many organizations get caught up in the trap of trying to manage far too many products and services.

Every product or service that a company offers needs to be designed, produced, marketed, sold, financed, and supported in some way. Every new or modified product or service creates a cascade of incremental work and expense in these areas, even when the change is relatively minor. For example, redesigning the package for a consumer product—even without changing the product itself—requires new engineering specifications, materials procurement, labeling, production procedures, scheduling, packaging and shipping standards, financial analysis and tracking, advertising, pricing, sales force communications and training, customer service procedures, and more. It's a tremendous amount of work—work that in most companies is multiplied many times over since new products and product variations are introduced on a regular basis.

What makes this dynamic even more complexifying is that most organizations add new products and product variations faster than they retire them. Once a product or service is in the marketplace and is being bought by customers, the offering is difficult to withdraw. A tacit promise has been made to customers—a promise that cannot easily be broken. Moreover, revenue is being produced, and goodwill is being generated, both of which are being used to fund the continuing operations of the organization—and most managers are hesitant to turn off this spigot in exchange for the uncertain and untested revenue streams that will come from the new products. As a result, the products and product variations that companies offer are constantly proliferating. This means that the organization is managing not only a constant stream of new product and service introductions, but also a growing base of existing products and services. This is the essence of volume complexity.

The real challenge of volume complexity, however, goes back to the "kid in the candy store" analogy—it involves making choices that are not always rational or easy. For example, on the one hand, managers are told to be entrepreneurial and creative and stay close to their markets—in other words, drive growth through constantly coming up with new ways of delighting customers. Many companies in fact have incentives for new product ideas and set goals for deriving a certain amount of revenue from new products. On the other hand, managers are also told to increase the sales volume of existing products and services, leverage the existing product and expense base, and build the brand and image of current offerings. So managers and employees (and customers) naturally develop emotional attachments to current products.

With these two sets of messages in mind, most companies avoid making choices. They keep the existing products and services, while also adding the new ones. And eventually this evolution becomes too costly and complex to sustain. For example, in 2008 Ford CEO Alan Mulally announced an ambitious product simplification effort, setting a goal of reducing the number of car "platforms" around the world by 40 percent in the following three years. This would increase engineering standardization, allow for significant purchasing savings, and make the whole enterprise less complex and costly—to the tune of billions of dollars. What was particularly interesting about the announcement, however, is that Mulally's predecessors at Ford had announced similar initiatives in the past—the most significant being the creation of what was called Ford's "world car." Although using different words, this earlier initiative also attempted to dramatically reduce product engineering and production variations on a global basis. Unfortunately, despite the good intentions, Ford's previous management had not been able to make the hard choices that the "world car" initiative required— forcing Mulally as the next CEO to try again.

Support Complexity: How Is This Supposed to Work?

If you've ever bought a product that included the phrase "some assembly required," then you probably understand the kind of complexity that can be created by product or service support. Whether high- or low-tech, most products and services require instructions or training for customers about how to put product pieces together, how to start using a product, how to derive the most benefit from a product, and then how to get help when something doesn't work or the instructions aren't clear. When this envelope of support is simple—as with a plug-and-play appliance—it can be a competitive advantage. When the support is unclear or overly complex—for example, when a customer is looking at a pile of parts that don't fit together—then support complexity can drain value from even the best of products.

We often forget that products need to be understood and used properly for customers to gain the intended benefits. Not long ago, I bought an electric razor that I thought was simple to use. After initially charging the battery (as per the instruction manual), I used the razor a number of times and was quite satisfied. After checking the instruction manual about whether the razor could be used with different electric currents, I took it on a trip to Europe and promptly fried the mechanism. Puzzled (and annoyed) by this development, I studied the instruction manual more carefully to understand what had happened—only to learn that the same instruction booklet was used for several models, some set up for universal current and some not. (Mine, of course, was not.) The instructions referred to the three model numbers, which differed by one letter each—and which were apparently on the original package but not on the razor itself. From the company's perspective, using the same instruction manual for several models of the same product probably saved money. But unintentionally, this made things more complex for the end user. The challenge for organizations is to think about how to simplify the wider context of their products and services—in addition to the offering itself. This includes the application, the instructions for use, and the ongoing help and support.

Several years ago, when Roger Servison was the head of retail marketing at Fidelity Investments, he spearheaded an effort to simplify the context of the mutual fund products as a way of growing investor market share. The old strategy for growth was to continually add funds with diverse investment strategies that would appeal to different classes of customers. Each mutual fund, however, was treated as a separate and distinct product, with its own application, statement, mailing schedule, and support mechanisms. The complexity of these support processes wasn't just costly—according to market research, it was actually inhibiting growth. Customers who wanted more than one product were being asked to submit the same information over and over, and they were being inundated with information from the different funds afterward.

To combat this complexity and improve Fidelity's share of the consumer wallet, Servison collaborated with other parts of the retail organization to sponsor projects that created a single application. The application was backed up by a consolidated statement, used coordinated and streamlined mailings (or e-mailings) of prospectuses and brochures, and offered more integrated (cross-fund) customer support. While it took several years to make all of these changes a reality, they eventually became standard practice in the mutual fund industry—and also fueled a period of rapid growth for Fidelity. Not one of the products was changed, but the simpler context in which they were all offered and supported made a significant difference.[2]

System Complexity: Putting Products Together

Several years ago, managers at the GE Healthcare business were puzzled by low customer satisfaction ratings, which didn't match their internal measures. From their perspective, products such as CAT (computer assisted tomography) scanners, MRI (magnetic resonance imaging) machines, and other kinds of medical imaging equipment were being delivered on time. Yet the customers were saying that the equipment was not up and running when they expected it to be. What was going on?

When GE troubleshooters X-rayed the problem (so to speak), they discovered that their equipment was indeed arriving on time—but many of the other components needed to make it operational were not. In other words, getting GE's product into the medical suite was only one part of the overall system. The rest of the system—the room construction, wiring, benches and tables, lights, and supplies—also needed to be in place. Otherwise, GE's product was essentially worthless. With this insight in mind, GE Healthcare worked with the other component suppliers so that together they would deliver a functioning system rather than a set of products that the customer would have to piece together.

System complexity is the extent to which your products and services must integrate with those of other suppliers to create value for a customer. Obviously, some products or services are stand-alone and don't need other products to function. But many are components that need to be combined or used with others in some way—and organizations need to pay attention to the complexity that this can create. For example, Cisco Systems is the leading supplier of routers, switches, and other equipment used by organizations to run their internal and external data, voice, and video information systems. As a technology company, Cisco is in the forefront of developing new features and capabilities that customers can use to improve the speed and reliability of their systems. The problem is that Cisco's equipment needs to be integrated into each customer's own customized network—which includes equipment from many vendors. So every time Cisco adds or changes something—no matter how good the reason—it could unintentionally interfere with the functioning of the network as a whole.

As Cisco has become more aware of this challenge, its engineers have placed attention not just on the improvement of its own products but also on the integration of its products with those of other vendors. For example, Cisco has created laboratories where it can simulate a customer network and then test the impact of new equipment and features on this network. While not perfect and not applicable to every situation, this is a step toward reducing system complexity for customers.

Design Complexity: Development from the Inside Out

Most people agree that Apple's iPod has become an icon of consumer electronics and the core of a multimedia revolution in telecommunications, music, video, photography, education, and lifestyle. But what is most instructive about the iPod is not its growing functionality and impact but how its success stems from the simplicity of its design. As one writer noted, "At the very moment the world of gadgets has become incredibly complicated, the iPod offers the serenity of simplicity."[3] It has virtually no buttons to push or complicated instructions; it fits in your hand or pocket; it puts the user in control of its contents and features; and it works seamlessly with other devices.

Design complexity yields the opposite of the iPod—products that are designed from an engineering perspective instead of an end-user one and that are therefore often difficult to use. We've all experienced the problem—phones with features we can't figure out or use; VCRs we can't see how to program; automobiles with buttons and switches we can't easily find.

But design complexity is not just about consumer products or electronics; it also applies to business-to-business products and services. For example, Intuit's Simple Start product—a basic accounting software package for small businesses—sold 100,000 units in its first year on the market. Simple Start began as a version of the company's core accounting product with fewer features. But its customers still found the software too hard to use and too full of accounting jargon, so Intuit's product team went back to the drawing board and focused on the small business owner's perspective. As business writer Linda Tischler describes: "Accounts receivable became 'money in' and accounts payable 'money out.' They pared back 125 setup screens to three and 20 major tasks to six essentials. They spent days worrying about the packaging, knowing that to this audience, something labeled 'Simple Accounting' was an oxymoron."[4] In other words, Intuit designed the product from the outside in—making something that the customer could experience as simple—instead of doing something that was simple from its own perspective.

Design complexity is often difficult for an organization to overcome, for several reasons. First, the lifeblood of most companies is innovation—new products or services. Therefore, people within a company often have the incentive to come up with the latest and greatest new feature, whether or not customers really want something new. Second, engineers, technologists, and other product designers are experts who often become enamored of their own creations and the elegance of their designs—and find it difficult to compromise that elegance for customers. And third, companies are often arrogant, or at least misguided, in thinking they know what their customers want better than the customers themselves. Taken together, these three factors cause organizations to design products that are far more complex than need be. As Tischler writes: "Blame the closed feedback loop among engineers and industrial designers, who simply can't conceive of someone so lame that she can't figure out how to download a ring tone; blame a competitive landscape in which piling on new features is the easiest way to differentiate products, even if it makes them harder to use; blame marketers who haven't figured out a way to make 'ease of use' sound hip."[5]

Given these factors, it takes a special kind of intelligence to counter design complexity and create simple designs with fewer features. It also takes humility to start with the customer's perspective rather than your own and to really listen to what people need. To tap into that kind of intelligence or to learn how to develop some measure of it, many companies have turned to design firms such as IDEO not only to design products for them, but also to teach managers how to develop the mind-set of design simplicity.[6] Others look for principles such as those provided by John Maeda, who ran MIT's Media Lab "Simplicity Consortium." He suggests that product simplification is a matter of "more is less"—fewer features, fewer buttons, fewer distractions—so that the customer can get the most out of the product.[7]

Overcoming Product-Related Complexity

The four sources of product-related complexity are deeply ingrained in organizations and in managerial behavior. As with structural complexity in an organization, managers do not set out to make products more numerous, complex, or hard to understand or assemble. From their perspective, it just sort of happens, as part of the normal course of events. The starting point for simplification, however, is to realize that product-related complexity doesn't "just happen." It's caused by the managerial dynamics described in this chapter—lack of disciplined choice-making, inside-out thinking, poor integration with other products and vendors, failure to listen to customers. Therefore, the solutions need to counter these dynamics. Managers can use three structured approaches to do just that:

1. Portfolio analysis

2. SKU rationalization and reduction

3. Customer design partnering

Portfolio Analysis

Perhaps the best-known approach to reducing product complexity is to engage in a strategic analysis of your company's products and services—and then use that analysis to make decisions about pruning or reshaping your portfolio. GE pioneered this thinking with its strategic business units in the 1970s. Bruce Henderson, one of the founders of the Boston Consulting Group (BCG), built on GE's work and popularized the approach in the 1980s; now most strategic consulting firms practice some variation on it.

The essence of portfolio analysis is to categorize products and services into buckets using financial and market data, plus fit with strategic goals. The buckets usually derive from some sort of matrix (most often two-by-two) that forces company managers to make hard choices about which products should be eliminated or divested, which should remain, and which should be supported or grown even more.

The classic BCG matrix looks like figure 3-1 and has evocative names for each category (which is one of the reasons why this model has become a standard for business).

As the matrix suggests, the stars—the products or services that should form the core of the company's business—already have a significant following and have even more growth prospects ahead. In contrast, the dogs have little current market share and poor prospects for future growth, and (using the BCG terminology) should be "shot"—that is, divested or eliminated. The cash cows—products with high market shares but little prospect of future growth—are worth keeping as long as they continue to pull in cash, but need to be watched for signs of moving into the dogs category.

FIGURE 3-1

The BCG "growth-share" model

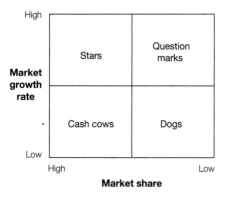

Source: Used with the permission of the Boston Consulting Group.

And question marks represent products that may have significant future potential but have not yet proved their worth—and thus pose questions about how much to risk on them.

Underlying this categorization is an assumption that products have a life cycle and potentially go through the stages in the matrix over time, as shown in figure 3-2. Thus, the categorization is not necessarily static; it needs to be redone periodically as products mature and the marketplace changes.

The power of this model is its simplicity—and that it forces senior managers to confront choices that they often prefer to avoid. It therefore often leads to intense debates about which products are really in which categories, which data to use for the categorization, which assumptions are behind the categorizations, and so on. These are all healthy debates, and they stem from the basic psychological issues discussed earlier: that managers feel loyalty and emotional commitment to their products, regardless of how long the products have been in the family.

FIGURE 3-2

Product life cycle

BCG positions throughout the product lifecycle

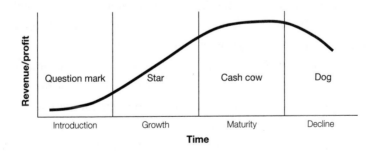

Source: Used with the permission of the Boston Consulting Group.

As noted, GE has used a variation on this model for many decades and applies it both at the business portfolio level and to products within its portfolio. For example, GE's plastics business in the 1980s and the first part of the 1990s was considered a star—a dominant, technology-based business with significant growth potential. Over time, as plastics became commoditized, the business turned into a cash cow. When petroleum-based raw materials escalated in cost, further eroding margins, the company—once a significant part of GE's growth engine—became a dog and was sold in 2006 to a Saudi Arabian company.

Sometimes the categorization of a business or products within the portfolio analysis not only sparks debate but also provokes innovation. For example, GE's retail credit card business was originally set up to help consumers buy GE appliances during the Depression. By the 1980s, the company was providing this credit by issuing and servicing branded credit cards on behalf of various retailers. When Jack Welch did his portfolio analysis in the early 1980s, the business appeared to be either a cash cow or a dog. Consumers were switching to universal credit cards—MasterCard, Visa, and others—and it appeared that the future for branded retail credit cards was bleak. The company was even put on the block, but no one else saw a future in it, either: no buyers stepped up. The head of the business at the time, David Eckdahl, then decided to rethink the business and its products and find a way of becoming more of a growth business with real prospects for the future. To do that, he shifted his focus away from consumers as the customer and more toward the retailer. With that focus, he rethought his entire product portfolio—creating many more products for helping retailers build sales, increase brand recognition, bring customers into their stores, improve their customer service, and more. All of a sudden, the company began to grow and its position within the GE portfolio changed—it became a star. Eventually, the international arm of the company was carved off into a separate company—called GE Money—that became, under the direction of David Nissen, one of GE's largest and most profitable businesses. But like all businesses with life cycles, GE Money began to experience a slowing of growth in 2007, and in the midst of the consumer credit crunch of 2008, it too became a target for divestment.[8]

SKU Rationalization and Reduction

The term *SKU* is short for "stock-keeping unit": a distinct and unique product or product variation, designated with a number. This ID system allows a company to track its wares from manufacturing through distribution to customers. Separate SKU numbers are usually given to even minor variations of the same product—for example a six-pack and an eight-pack, a special promotional package design, or a country-specific formulation. As companies tailor and customize products and promotions, SKUs proliferate like leaves sprouting from branches that represent the core products. While product portfolio analysis might prune whole branches of the product tree, SKU rationalization and reduction is meant to thin the leaves.

SKU analysis is often initiated from a functional perspective because of the complexity that large numbers of SKUs create for manufacturing, distribution, sales, and all the support areas. For example, the European manufacturing division of a global pharmaceutical company worked with consulting firm BCG to assess the impact of its SKU variations on plant complexity and related costs. Using the data summarized in figure 3-3, managers discovered that 20 percent of plant costs resulted from the changeovers and short-run batches required by having so many product variations. This led the managers to undertake an SKU rationalization program,

FIGURE 3-3

Impact of SKU proliferation

High product complexity—numerous low-volume SKUs, low average batch size

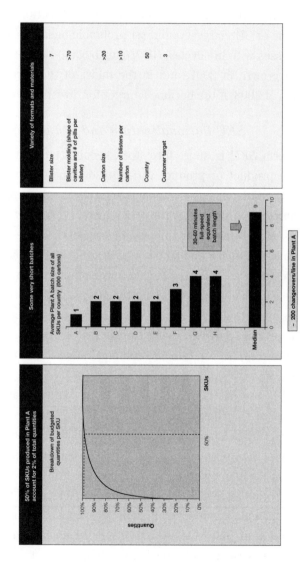

Source: Used with the permission of the Boston Consulting Group.

examining each variation from a country and regulatory stand-point—a program that eventually helped reduce operating costs significantly in each plant.[9]

Few companies realize the extent to which SKUs proliferate and how much complexity and cost can result. In fact, many managers actively encourage proliferation as a way of providing more customer choice and customization. They don't see that the resulting complexity can actually be harmful, both to company profitability and to customer satisfaction. The Aeron chair is a case in point.

Winner of the prestigious Design of the Decade award in 1999 and named in 2002 as among the fifteen best-designed consumer products of the past hundred years, the Aeron chair is one of manufacturer Herman Miller's most recognizable and best-selling products.[10] Chairs, however, are very personal items, and one of the most powerful selling points of the Aeron chair is its ability to "adapt naturally and adjust precisely to fit people of all sizes and postures doing all kinds of activities, all day long."[11] In other words, the Aeron chair allows its user to make all sorts of personal adjustments in the basic product. In addition to the flexibility built into the design, however, Herman Miller offers nineteen steps a customer can take to customize the chair at time of purchase: size, colors, materials, and other features, with multiple choices for each step.

For many years, Herman Miller's product design and marketing people assumed that the more choice they could give consumers, the better. However, when Mary Stevens became senior vice president of product management in 2007, she began to think about the implications of this assumption. She discovered that the nineteen customization steps resulted in a massive proliferation of SKUs. In reality, the company was offering customers 140 million configurations of the Aeron chair and had to be prepared to manufacture every one of those possibilities.

As Stevens and her team explored this further, they realized that this SKU complexity had significant operational and cost consequences. For example, because of all the onetime configurations, the supplier that provided the Pellicle (mesh) suspension material for the chair was having to dedicate 80 percent of its manufacturing capacity to only 20 percent of its output—a significant inefficiency. Similarly, the systems and finance departments were maintaining extensive price files for each possible SKU, and marketing was continually preparing new collateral material. What was most stunning about this, however, was that consumers didn't really value all the choice that Herman Miller was providing. Of the 140 million possible configurations, only 4,000 were actually ordered with any frequency—with fewer than 400 configurations providing the majority of bulk sales.

With this data in hand, Stevens initiated a significant SKU reduction effort—trimming down to ten the number of customization steps involved in buying a chair, and also reducing the options within each step. Using customer input—what she describes as an "outside-in perspective"—her eventual goal is to reduce the number of possible configurations to less than 200,000.

Customer Design Partnering

As Mary Stevens's simplification of the Aeron chair illustrates, one of the keys to reducing product complexity is to develop more of an external mind-set, thinking from the outside in. Developing this kind of mentality has always been a challenge for companies—it's always easier to make things first and then take them to market. The assumption behind this way of thinking is that we (the company and its technologists and designers) know what you (the customer or consumer) need, and we've designed the product to meet those needs. Now we just need to convince you—through advertising, promotion, education, incentives, and the like—to agree.

Unfortunately, when products, designs, and promotions are off the mark, companies often create more variations or bells and whistles—hoping that they will get lucky and truly meet customers' needs. Alternatively, they increase advertising and promotion, which—like talking louder to someone who speaks a foreign language—is actually annoying and unlikely to increase understanding.

The simplest route to a successful product or service is not usually by pushing it through advertising, promotion, and sales, but by offering designs that customers want badly enough to pull from the company's shelves voluntarily. One of the ways to create this pull is to engage the customer directly in the design process.

Cisco Systems is a good example of how engaging customers in structured and intentional ways can make a difference. Cisco has at least three separate mechanisms for doing this. First, as mentioned earlier in this chapter, one of the jobs of Cisco's product test laboratories is to replicate aspects of customers' networks to show how the company's products function in the customer's environment. Its engineers and marketers realize that their products not only must be reliable and effective in their own right, but also must work in conjunction with the other products that make up the customer's network. Otherwise, as Cisco has learned from its customers, its products unintentionally make its customers' networks more complex and difficult to manage.

A second way that Cisco engages customers is through its Executive Business Centers (EBCs). These are product demonstration sites that Cisco has set up in major locations around the world. They provide a setting where customers can come in and "kick the tires" on both networking and advanced technology products. The centers also serve as the backdrop for intense dialogues between Cisco people and teams of customers about products, services, and how Cisco can best meet customers' needs. Each EBC also has a "telepresence" room (Cisco's real-time, high-definition, video communication system) so that customers can talk with Cisco experts almost anywhere in the world.

In addition to these mechanisms, Cisco asks customers to serve on a number of advisory boards. Some boards are organized by customer segment (for example, large global enterprises); others focus on technologies (such as security). In all cases, customer organizations nominate key people (as many as twenty-five per board, some at very senior levels) to participate in formal meetings at least twice a year, with subgroup or individual advisory work in between. The job of these boards is to provide feedback on new products, to identify needs for Cisco to meet, and to generally give Cisco guidance about product road maps, features, and investments (including ideas about acquisitions of small start-up technology companies).[12] A typical mission statement for a Cisco advisory board reads like this: "Our mission is to provide an executive-level forum to accelerate Cisco's delivery of programs and services to meet the specific needs of our customers. We are committed to listening to our customers and understanding what is required to help our customers' business and technical leaders achieve their goals."

In this context, one of these advisory boards spent several sessions over the course of eighteen months helping Cisco's product engineers and technology leaders explore what it would mean to achieve "extreme"—perfect—network availability. During the advisory board meetings, sessions focused on how to improve product quality, how to strengthen network security and availability, and how to manage network complexity. In between, Cisco staff followed up on feedback and inputs from board members so that progress could be reported at the next meeting.

While each customer advisory board session adds value, the real message here is the overall commitment that Cisco has to partnering with its customers on its offerings. As an organization, Cisco

spends many millions of dollars and employs a large number of managers and staff whose main job is to make sure that Cisco listens to its customers systematically, even when the message is not something pleasant to hear. According to Patrick Finn, a vice president who has run several sales businesses for Cisco, "the commitment to customer engagement keeps us focused on what's important so that we don't get caught up in the complexity of all the new technologies."

These kinds of customer input mechanisms make sense for technology products, and they also work for other industries and product categories. For example, Fidelity Investments uses "customer laboratories" as a way of getting feedback on new products and how easy they are to use and understand. When Fidelity was developing a Web-based retirement planning service, the company brought in customers from different demographic and economic segments to explore the tool and provide feedback. Similarly, Philips Electronics has a "simplicity advisory board" made up of outside experts who help the company create simplified offerings such as instruction manuals that non-tech-savvy consumers can understand.

Product Simplification: A Challenge That Never Ends

Overcoming product proliferation and complexity is an ongoing challenge, not a onetime simplification exercise. Every firm, whether for-profit or not, needs to develop and offer products and services that meet customer needs. To do this, executives inevitably encourage not only the expansion of existing products and services but also the constant development of new ones. Taken together, these two objectives unintentionally create product complexity—either from having too many products or from having products that don't fit easily into the customers' social or technical environment, or from some combination of these factors.

To counter product complexity, simplicity-minded managers need to periodically or continually address the complexity questions raised in this chapter: *Are we offering too many products and services to our customers? Are we making it hard for our customers to understand and use our products and services? Are we designing our products and services so that they can't be easily integrated with other products that the customer may use in conjunction with them? Are we missing ways to build more simplicity into the design of our products and services?*

If your answers to any of these questions suggest that product complexity is an issue, then you may need a structured methodology to help you choose which products to offer, how many features to build into products, and how to design your products and services from the customer's outside-in point of view. The approaches described in this chapter—product portfolio analysis, SKU rationalization and reduction, and customer-design partnering—are meant to help you do that.

Like any set of tools, however, these approaches are only as effective as the hand that puts them to use. Driving toward product simplicity requires persistence and vigilance, a willingness to make tough choices, and an ability to really see the world from your customer's perspective. Simplicity doesn't come easily. But having the right number of the right products at the right times is a wonderful prescription for organizational success—and is certainly worth the effort.

FOUR

Streamlining Processes

Processes represent the steps and sequence for getting things done—ranging from the strategic (such as designing and commercializing new products) to the tactical (expense reporting) to the mundane (ordering more paper for the printer). When these processes take more steps than necessary, or are unclear, or have too many people involved at the wrong times, they become major sources of complexity. This chapter discusses how processes become overly complex—and what managers can do to steer them toward simplicity instead.

The Challenge of Process Complexity

When Thomas Kirsch was named global head of quality assurance (QA) for Johnson & Johnson's R&D enterprises in early 2000, he wasn't quite sure what he had gotten himself into. As head of QA for the Pharmaceutical Research Institute (PRI), which is Johnson &

Johnson's U.S. R&D organization, Kirsch had worked hard to build a highly effective group carrying out standard processes for auditing and reporting on quality, monitoring the quality of clinical trials, setting up new suppliers, and quickly fixing other quality problems. But PRI was only one of several research organizations in the Johnson & Johnson family, and his remit now included the Janssen Research Foundation (JRF) in Europe and Johnson & Johnson's Asian R&D operations. Traditionally, these organizations had been fiercely independent. Even though owned by Johnson & Johnson for many years, they produced their own products in their own ways. As the pharmaceutical business became more global, however—with drugs discovered, manufactured, and distributed in different parts of the world, and government regulators increasingly cooperating with one another—this pattern had to change. Kirsch was charged with making it happen from a QA perspective. And to make life just a little more challenging, demands for audits and compliance were increasing faster than available budget or trained personnel, so Kirsch also had to significantly improve the overall productivity of the QA function at the same time.

Kirsch quickly realized that the key to success would be process simplification and standardization. Even PRI's three U.S. QA sites all did things slightly differently, which made it hard to combine resources and standardize reporting; adding two sites in Europe and one in Asia would make it even harder. However, just telling everyone to do things the same way, with a single template and set of instructions, wouldn't work, either. Each unit had developed its own ways of working according to local needs and conditions, and its people were hardly going to give up decades of successful practice just because a new boss had been dropped in from corporate headquarters. At best they would listen respectfully and then spend their time "educating" the new guy about why they needed to do things the way they did.

Given this reality, Kirsch decided to engage as many people as possible, across the sites, in an ongoing QA "integration and simplification" initiative. First he brought together his new leadership team—managers from all six sites—to understand the business imperatives and the benefits of QA integration and to catalog the major processes that constituted the QA function. The team then selected several work processes for immediate focus: auditing clinical trials, getting ready for regulators' visits to manufacturing sites, and following up on the closure of previously identified audit exceptions. These would all make a material difference if they were done as common, simple, global processes—in terms of cost reduction and resource utilization, knowledge sharing, or risk mitigation.

Kirsch and his managers then appointed teams representing all the QA locations to focus on these three processes. At a three-day workshop in Belgium, the teams mapped out how the processes were done in different parts of the world, debated the pros and cons of the different approaches, and settled on a recommended "global process" that had to meet several criteria: achieve or exceed regulatory requirements, have one optimized process for all of global QA, and get the work done faster and more easily than before. Toward the end of the workshop, the teams presented their recommendations to Kirsch and his managers, who debated and refined the recommendations before accepting them. The teams were then given one hundred days to put these new processes in place across the entire Johnson & Johnson organization. This meant that they had to write standard operating procedures, design and implement training plans, and communicate all the changes to the affected staff (both within QA and in related R&D areas).

In light of the success of the first wave of process simplification, Kirsch and his management team commissioned new teams every four months. Over the course of two years, all the QA processes were globalized and simplified, and almost every member of the QA function had participated in at least one team. This widespread participation made acceptance of the new processes relatively smooth, since these were changes that the staff was developing themselves and not having imposed on them. It also gave the QA staff a much broader global perspective on the business and helped them build relationships with colleagues around the world—so that process simplification became a way of life and not an unusual event. Thus, when Johnson & Johnson expanded the remit of Kirsch's organization to include Centocor, the company's major biotechnology arm, in 2002, it was relatively easy to bring the new area into the QA fold and to do the same with a continuing string of acquisitions in the years that followed. More important, the overall productivity of the QA function worldwide increased by 50 percent over the four years from 2000 to 2004.

How Process Evolution Unintentionally Adds to Complexity

As Johnson & Johnson's experience illustrates, unless process complexity is addressed systematically, it adds to costs, makes it difficult to get things done effectively and quickly, and can get in the way of major strategic initiatives such as globalizing R&D. But nobody intentionally designs processes to be complex and convoluted or delights in making it difficult to get things done. Rather, processes evolve over time, becoming complex in four ways:

- *Local differences:* As organizations evolve, the same processes are often done differently in different places. Sometimes, good initial reasons drive the variations, but the same work ends up getting done in different ways long after those reasons dissipate.

- *Multiplication of steps and loops:* As they encounter unique or recurring problems, processes tend to acquire more steps, more controls, and more people in the pursuit of solutions. Such solutions are rarely abandoned, and the accretion of steps and people continues unchecked until the process takes too long to complete.

- *Informality of process:* A third source of complexity is lack of rigor about how a process really is supposed to be carried out. Usually this absence of discipline comes about because people don't realize at first that the job they are doing is actually a replicable process. Over time, the unique ways that they do things settle in and become routine, even if these steps are not necessarily the best ways to proceed.

- *Lack of cross-functional or cross-unit transparency:* People naturally tend to focus on their part of the process rather than the whole, never realizing that work crosses many organizational lines, with dependencies and inter-dependencies throughout. As a result, the work of one unit often fails to dovetail with the work of the next.

To Each His Own: Local Differences Make Processes More Complex

Anyone who has lived in different countries around the world knows that local variations often make simple activities seem difficult. Shopping for food in your home country is usually easy and straightforward, for example—you know where to go, how to get there, what to buy, how to pay for it, and how to get it home. But try to perform that same process in a foreign country, and you have to think about every step along the way—where to find the local markets, what types of foods you can get in each store, how to figure prices in local currency, how shopkeepers and vendors expect you to act, and more.

Organizations with multiple locations, even in the same country—even in the same building—present similar challenges. If each office or unit does things differently, it's tough to operate as one company. People from one location feel like foreigners when they have to work in another—like the New York–based lawyer who recently told me how difficult it was when a case took him to his firm's Philadelphia office. The support, research, and documentation processes were so different there that he felt lost—even though the offices were little more than an hour apart by train.

Finding the right balance between locally autonomous processes and globally consistent processes is an ongoing struggle for most organizations. Global consistency makes it easier to share resources and move people from one location to another, fosters consistent measurements and makes it possible to compare performance across units, and is usually more cost-efficient. On the other hand, local processes often make it easier for a company to respond quickly to changing market conditions, consumer requirements, and competitive situations. The interplay between global and local processes is the essence of what Christopher Bartlett and Sumantra Ghoshal call the "transnational organization," in which some core processes, such as basic research or executive staffing, are done centrally and consistently while other processes like marketing and pricing are done locally.[1] Another term for this melding of local and global processes is what my colleague and former Harvard Business School professor Todd Jick calls a "glocal" organization: one that merges global processes with a respect for local presence. He likens it to a jazz ensemble with players from around the world, some playing together and some playing solos.[2]

Pfizer's Global Operations Division—which manages the company's facilities, real estate, travel, equipment maintenance, environmental safety, and other administrative services—is a good example of this process tension. Before Paul Begin took over the division in 2006, Pfizer's business units, functions, and locations more or less managed their own operations with some sharing of best practices through a global network. To reduce costs and reduce process complexity, Begin and his leadership team developed a set of consistent global processes for the company's major operational activities. For example, instead of allowing each business unit the authority to buy or lease its own office equipment, Global Operations created a set of common or regional standards, vendor contracts, and review processes. Thus, instead of every manager in every location having whatever equipment they wanted, standards were established for whether managers would have shared or private printers, color or black-and-white, and one vendor or another, etc. As these common processes were implemented across the globe, the company saved hundreds of millions of dollars while also simplifying its operational processes. However, making this happen required intense analysis and debate about each process, one at a time, to determine the costs, benefits, and trade-offs of global or regional standardization and local customization (and to deal with local resistance to giving up control)—with some decisions even escalated to the senior executive leadership team.

Local process variations—and increased cost and complexity—are inevitable as organizations grow and evolve. Creative managers are always looking for new, faster, and otherwise better ways of getting things done and in fact are usually rewarded for doing so. At the same time, conditions will always vary from location to location—with different workforce skills, cost structures, suppliers, customers, and competitors. Managers are compelled and drawn therefore to tailor their approaches to be successful. In addition, companies often grow through acquisitions of new units, locations, and personnel—and these new groups bring their own process variations. Keeping this constant entropy of processes under control is a major challenge for simplification.

Never Make the Same Mistake Once: Adding Steps and Loops Makes Processes More Complex

Early in my consulting career, I worked with the loan department of what was then the JP Morgan Bank. In those days, before totally computerized record keeping, many of the loans were documented in ledger books and payments were entered manually. All the clerks used pencils as part of their work (although official entries were in ink). In addition to the tedium of the manual entries, I was struck by the fact that the clerks had to keep track of their pencils and that when one pencil wore down, they needed to go to the "pencil lady" on the floor, show her the old pencil, and then receive a new one. When I asked why this procedure was needed, I was told that it was the only way to make sure that the clerks didn't waste pencils or take them home with them. The managers never seemed to notice that the clerical time absorbed by this process cost the company far more than it would have spent on any imaginable number of pencils.

Now fast-forward to a GE industrial business a number of years later. In this business, the lathe operators had to wear heavy rubber gloves to protect their hands as they worked high-speed lathes. Over time, when the gloves wore out, the operators needed to shut down their stations, walk over to another building, fill out a form, show their old gloves to a materials clerk, and only then be issued new gloves before walking back to work. It seemed like déjà vu when one of my colleagues asked why this procedure was used and was told that several years earlier, a box of gloves had gone missing. Again, it didn't seem to register that the value of box after box of gloves was evaporating in the human and machine downtime required to control them.

These examples seem silly in retrospect, but they illustrate how processes are constantly retooled to reduce risks and prevent problems—but in so doing are made increasingly cumbersome, expensive, and complex. One of the important managerial tasks is to make sure that problems are not only solved but prevented from recurring. To keep problems from repeating themselves, therefore, managers add steps or controls to their standard processes. Over time, these additional steps become institutionalized. The tradition then continues long after anyone remembers how it started or what its original purpose was.

One of the ways that managers can simplify processes is to periodically challenge steps that have gone unquestioned for many years, to ask why the step is being done, and to explore whether it still adds value or is necessary. For example, a GE leasing business was exploring how to speed up the process for liquidating assets that come off lease. As part of examining the process, managers questioned whether the regional manager needed to sign off on all the associated paperwork, or whether it could be done by the branch managers alone. The acid test for this question was whether the regional managers actually added any value to the process, or whether their signature was just a rubber stamp. In analyzing the question, the branch managers discovered that the regional managers had never disallowed a lease liquidation proposal, or changed the price, or done anything else to change the transaction. According to that data, it was a no-brainer to eliminate the regional managers' involvement in the process.[3]

Often these extra control points, signatures, or reviews exist because managers at all levels feel that they are accountable for costs, quality, and results, which is a natural and good thing. In that context, they don't want anyone to think that they haven't put their two cents in, that they don't know what's going on, or that they aren't "in control" of the situation. This focus on control is based on the hierarchical notion that all information needs to flow up the chain of command for approval. Often however, the more high-level approvals there are, the further the managers are from the real data and the ability to actually add value. So not only are the reviews and controls not worth much, but they also slow down the process and reduce the empowerment and sense of accountability of the people closer to the decision. In fact, when there are many layers of approval, people on the ground may not give an issue the proper attention, because they assume that someone further up the line will catch anything they miss.

Managers also frequently add steps to prevent potential problems. When managers or their organizations are particularly risk-averse, these preventive measures can sometimes become onerous. At the New York Federal Reserve Bank, one of the managers once commented that the basic purpose of process management at the Fed was to not let the same mistake happen once—that is, to think about every possible contingency and plan a way to deal with it. Obviously, this is impossible, but it sounds like a useful goal even though all it usually does is add process complexity. For example, Gary Rodkin, CEO of ConAgra Foods, tells the story of when he was a new product manager at General Mills many years ago: he was told to prepare for product reviews by identifying and answering in advance (with full data analysis) every question that senior management *might* ask. This level of preparation of course took weeks, and 90 percent of the data was never used. A simpler approach, which he now employs with his own product managers, is to have them prepare only for the obvious questions—and to research afterward any questions that can't be answered on the spot.

Paving Over the Cow Paths: How Process Informality Causes Complexity

If you've ever wondered why the streets of Boston and other New England towns meander so much, it's because these routes were originally cow paths. Over time, as the cows followed the same paths from barn to grazing area, these paths were beaten down and eventually became established roads. Today these cow paths are paved, named, and marked on maps as the authorized way to get from one place to another, and we rarely question why we are taking such a circuitous route. They also are very hard to change or straighten out because buildings, utility lines, and other kinds of infrastructure have grown up around them.

Many processes in organizations have much the same genesis. Instead of being intentionally designed, they have evolved through happenstance, tradition, and repetition to a point where they go unquestioned. Whatever inefficiency was built in over the years becomes institutionalized as a cost of doing business. Having lots of these inefficient, unplanned, and meandering processes in place is a natural source of complexity—forcing people to take more time and work harder to get things done.

Here's a quick illustration: GE's finance arm, GE Capital, made many acquisitions in the early 1990s, as many as fifty a year at one point. To achieve this kind of volume, GE developed highly efficient processes for what it called "business development," which included searching out acquisition targets, doing due diligence on them, developing valuation and pricing models, negotiating terms and conditions, and closing the deals. Each step along the way included a series of playbooks and checklists, and the business development staffs, lawyers, and finance people were all well trained in using them effectively. So far, so good.

The only problem with this system was that it stopped once the deals were done. The business development team would close a deal, then just assume that the appropriate business unit or operations team (GE Capital had more than twenty businesses) would take it from there. So while the front end of doing the deal had a disciplined process, the back end of integrating the deal, including measuring the results and holding people accountable for them, was completely informal. No one even thought about it as a replicable process. As a result, some of the deals paid off—but many did not.

Given the amount of investment that GE was making in new companies, this random and informal way of integrating acquisitions eventually became unacceptable. To straighten out the informal cow paths that the business units had created, GE Capital's senior human resource leader, Larry Toole, commissioned a team to develop a standard and replicable process for integration. Led by one of his key people, Larry DeMonaco, the team interviewed dozens of people involved in GE Capital's earlier acquisitions—on both sides of the deal—to identify key lessons, what worked, and what needed to be included in the integration process. Using the interview and other performance data, they then brought together people from all the different GE Capital businesses in a series of working conferences to hammer out a common process, which eventually became known as the GE Pathfinder Model, for acquisition integration.[4] Eventually, this model became the basis for GE's integration playbook, spelling out key roles (such as an integration manager) and nonnegotiable steps that were necessary for success—and helping GE achieve much better results from its acquisitions.

GE Capital's experience shows how major processes such as acquisition integration can be treated informally, not even recognized for what they are. But many smaller day-to-day processes create complexity the same way. At a Work-Out session with Walmart a number of years ago, a store manager raised the question of how customers' personal checks were approved at the stores. It turns out that at the time, checkout clerks would need to ask for identification and then either walk the check over to a store manager (or assistant) or have the manager come to them. While this transportation of eight-foot fluorescent bulbs, which were placed on wooden pallets for shipping. The manufacturing people discovered that if they lashed two four-foot pallets together, it would be less expensive than using a single eight-foot pallet. So after careful study, they implemented this change and took credit for the cost reduction.

While manufacturing was focusing on cost reduction, the customer-service function was trying to reduce the number of returns—bulbs that customers brought back because they were broken or defective. These returns not only lost the company goodwill and replacement costs, but also entailed crediting accounts, posting additional transactions, and transporting the broken materials and disposing of them. What neither function realized, however, was that manufacturing's cost-reduction activities were actually increasing the volume of returns. It turned out that manufacturing was using eight-foot forklifts to move the pallets (which were shrink-wrapped) onto trucks. But the warehouse and shipping areas were using four-foot forklifts—so when they lifted the bundles, one of the lashed-together pallets was separated from the other by a few inches, and the bottom row of bulbs was often broken. Because of the shrink-wrap, this breakage was not apparent—until customers unwrapped the packages and discovered it.

Looking at the total end-to-end process, it is obvious that manufacturing's actions were counterproductive. Saving a few cents on each pallet was costing many millions of dollars in returned goods, complex accounting, and lost goodwill. But as in many organizations, people weren't looking at the overall process, only their piece of it. And from its own perspective, manufacturing was doing all the right things.

As with the other sources of process complexity, poor cross-functional coordination is not intentional or malicious; one division of the organization does not usually aim to make work more

was happening, the customer would get uncomfortable ("
they questioning my credit?") and the lines would gro
everyone waited for the manager's approval—which was
always forthcoming; very few checks were ever disallowed.
the process over, the Work-Out group realized that the stor
ager didn't really add value to the process. As a result, W
revised its process (which it didn't know was a replicable pr
so that the checkout clerk could quickly verify the shopper's i
fication with a driver's license or other ID and then approv
transaction. This simpler process improved customer service
out raising losses.

Every organization has multitudes of processes, big and si
that evolve over time without much thought or discipline. Strai
ening out these cow-path processes is a major opportunity
simplification.

The Boat's Not Leaking in My End: Lack of Cross-Functional Transparency

The *New Yorker* once ran a wonderful cartoon: four people sit in
rowboat; two are bailing furiously while the boat tips in their direc
tion, inspiring the high and dry pair to comment, "Sure glad the
hole's not in our end."

Over the years, this cartoon has elicited not only smiles from
managers but also many comments about how some siloed and disconnected processes cause undue complexity in their companies.
When one part of the company is going north and another is going
south, the overall route is bound to be circuitous and may not even
lead to the desired destination.

Here's a good illustration: several years ago at GE Lighting, the
manufacturing function worked very hard to improve the cost-
efficiency of its processes. One opportunity involved the storage and

difficult and more complex for others. These misalignments, rather, come from lack of visibility of the overall end-to-end process. The units fail to understand or consider the downstream implications of their actions. In concert with this missing transparency, differing incentives and goals also foster misalignment. In the GE Lighting case, manufacturing's primary goal was cost reduction, whereas the customer service function focused on customer satisfaction. While these goals are not at all incompatible, they do require coordination and possible trade-offs. By increasing its own costs, manufacturing would not only improve customer service but also reduce overall costs in the business.

Five Tools for Process Simplification

The four sources of process complexity described in this chapter are constantly at work to some degree in almost every organization. That's the bad news.

The good news is that a number of powerful and effective tools and approaches have been developed in recent years specifically to combat process complexity. While all these tools should be part of your simplification toolkit, they differ on several dimensions—speed, degree of technical rigor, and the extent to which they engage people in problem solving. As a start, this chapter describes five of these tools:

1. Best-practice identification

2. Process mapping and redesign

3. Six Sigma and Lean

4. Rapid results

5. Work-Out

Best-Practice Identification:
Sharing and Comparing

A first tool for simplifying processes is to look at how they are done in different places and then select the approach that fits your situation.[5] This can be done across different units of the same company, across two or more companies, or across an industry, and it can be done with a specific process or a set of related processes.

Within a company, a best-practices approach is particularly useful for highlighting and reducing local differences that have evolved over time or come in with mergers and acquisitions. For example, when ING's U.S. retirement services business bought the record-keeping company CitiStreet in 2008, CEO Kathy Murphy, HR head Randy Bailin, and the rest of the executive team realized that the two companies had different processes for serving key market segments, for prioritizing new products, and for handling customer service issues. Instead of insisting that CitiStreet simply adopt ING's practices or allowing different practices to continue, teams were formed to identify and understand the differences, assess the pros and cons, and develop recommendations for one process or the other, or some combination. This approach quickly led to a reduction of local differences, with some processes being adopted from each side—which made it easier to integrate CitiStreet into ING.

Across companies, best-practice sharing often suggests opportunities for making informal processes more rigorous or disciplined. When GE's corporate executive council met with Walmart's senior executives several years ago, it learned about Walmart's "quick market intelligence" process for the rapid capture and assessment of market data. GE, which did not have a formal way of doing this, quickly adapted the process to fit its own business model.

Here are some ways to go about best-practice identification and sharing:

- Assign teams to research the different practices and develop recommendations.

- Bring together managers from different areas or companies to share practices.

- Send managers on field visits to different locations.

- Hire outside experts or researchers to do the legwork.

No matter how it is done, the greatest value of a best-practice approach is to trigger learning about alternative processes. That background enables the company to make explicit decisions about ways to make the process as simple and effective as possible.

In general, best-practice identification can be done quickly; it takes little preparation or setup time, and the comparison of practices seldom require a lot of technical rigor or detailed data. It just needs participants who are involved in the process or know enough about it to describe what happens in fairly broad terms so that basic comparisons can be made. If more rigor or detail is then required, other tools can be employed. Depending on how it is done, best-practice identification can be highly engaging, at least for those directly involved in the exploration and discussion.

Process Mapping and Redesign: Making the Implicit Explicit

To simplify a process, you need to know what it looks like—what steps are involved, how they are sequenced, who carries them out.[6] In some cases—such as core manufacturing or engineering processes—this information is written down in procedural manuals and other documents. But in many cases, the actual process is opaque. People who are involved may understand their piece of it, but nobody has a holistic view. And without a common understanding of how a process actually works, attempts to simplify or improve it may feel like grasping at fog—you know something is there, but can't quite get hold of it.

Process mapping is a critical tool for making opaque processes visible so that they can be assessed and redesigned. It is a structured approach for documenting the key activities, decision points, timing, interdependencies, and players—with relatively simple graphics that give everyone a shared view of the process, and it can be applied to all four sources of process complexity. Process mapping can highlight local differences; it can explicitly call out extra loops and steps that have become institutionalized; it can map informal cow paths; and it can help create end-to-end transparency in processes that cut across functions and business areas.

Although process mapping can be done in great detail, it is usually most effective when kept at a relatively high level. The approach is also most effective when done in a way that engages the various stakeholders and enables them to talk with one another about it.

For example, when ConAgra wanted to simplify the process of developing advertisements for branded products, it brought together product managers, creative writers, media buyers, consumer researchers, finance managers, and others—both from within the company and from partner ad agencies. With the help of one of my colleagues, the participants wrote down on sticky notes all the steps that were involved. The participants placed these notes on a wall chart and then moved them around to capture the actual sequence of events—including go/no-go decisions, presentations, waiting time, and other aspects of how things really worked. The result of this "as-is" view of the current process was a myriad of steps, many of them redundant, scattered across the chart and linked up to one another in various ways. Below this view, the team members sketched out the "to-be" process that they wanted to create—cutting out loops and extra steps to reduce the overall time by many weeks.

The main value of process mapping is to allow stakeholders— all of whom see the process from different vantage points—to develop a common view of what's currently being done and what might be done differently. With this objective in mind, process mapping can be carried out quickly, and ideally with high degrees of engagement and medium levels of technical rigor. If it's necessary, additional rigor can be added—for example, team members can assess how much volume is involved at particular steps, or they can drill deeper down into more detailed substeps.

Process maps can be the starting point for reengineering efforts that are more analytical. In such cases, the process map generated by a cross-functional team is then given to a task group that analyzes each of the steps in greater depth, measures time and resources allotted to them, and eventually develops a reengineered process map. While this kind of data-driven, analytical approach can be very powerful, it also has the danger of disenfranchising the stakeholders. If people feel disengaged from the development of the new process, they are often inclined to resist it—making the implementation more difficult and sometimes actually causing it to fail.

Six Sigma and Lean: The Full Monty

Over the long term, perhaps the most effective way to drive process simplification is to reduce or eliminate variation.[7] If a process is stable and predictable, it is simpler to manage and to improve. That is the ultimate objective of Six Sigma and Lean approaches.

Six Sigma refers to the achievement of less than six standard deviations (the Greek letter sigma, σ, is the statistical symbol for standard deviation) from the mean in an ongoing process. In practice, that would be fewer than 3.4 defects or errors out of a million chances—which is close to perfect quality. It's like hitting a golf ball a million times—and having it travel the same yardage down the middle of the fairway on all but four swings.

As a process simplification methodology, Six Sigma was developed by Joseph M. Juran and W. Edwards Deming, two American engineers, when they were invited to Japan in the aftermath of World War II to help Japanese industry learn how to produce high-quality products so that "made in Japan" would not mean cheap and shoddy. The success of their Japanese acolytes was so stunning that by the 1970s, Japanese automakers had overtaken their American counterparts in terms of quality, cost, and speed to market. Many other industries soon followed suit, which caused U.S. and other Western companies, starting with Motorola, to adopt Six Sigma approaches of their own. Since the 1990s, thousands of organizations of all shapes and sizes in all industries have turned to Six Sigma tools to drive process improvement.

Lean is a methodology for process simplification that focuses on reducing wasted time, movement, and steps in process flows. Originally applied to manufacturing operations, it has been widely used to eliminate non-value-added steps and reduce the cost of complexity in support and service processes. One of its attractions is the potential for rapid deployment through what is called a Kaizen event, where people involved in a process work together intensively for three to five days to actually reshape the process (or even move the equipment in a manufacturing plant). More recently, Lean and Six Sigma have been combined, or employed in combination, as Lean Six Sigma.

Organizations that deploy Lean, Six Sigma, or Lean Six Sigma approaches usually train internal consultants with different levels of expertise and experience to be "green belts," "black belts," and "master black belts." These internal experts then work with managers and teams on specific simplification and improvement projects throughout the firm.

For example, the North Shore-LIJ Health System, which includes more than fifteen separate hospitals and other heath-care institutions and is the largest employer on Long Island, developed a large-scale Six Sigma effort that started in 2002. Over a five-year period, the centralized Center for Learning and Innovation trained dozens of managers and health-care professionals in Six Sigma tools. As part of the training, each person worked on a specific process simplification and improvement project under the supervision of master black belts. These experts initially came from the outside, but eventually were homegrown. During this time, ten waves of projects covered more than ninety different processes across the system—with each one aimed at accomplishing specific, measurable improvements through the reduction of process variation. Two illustrations will show how this worked.

Using operating rooms efficiently is a major challenge for hospitals since most hospitals have a limited operating-room capacity. The rooms are filled by both scheduled and emergency surgeries, and the duration or occurrence of the latter is often difficult to predict. From both a financial and a patient care standpoint, it is therefore important that the space be allocated in the best possible way. To make a difference in this area, one project focused on improving adherence to the scheduled starting time for the first case in each room on a given day—to improve the chances of avoiding or reducing backup later in the day. To do this, the team identified and eliminated frequent sources of delay, developed new approaches to booking the rooms, and created measures for tracking progress. The result was a reduction in late starts from an average of 17.6 minutes (with a standard deviation of 11 minutes) to an average of 4.8 minutes (with a standard deviation of 4 minutes).

Getting patients admitted and into a room may sound simple, but in reality it involves a great deal of complexity and variability— making sure that rooms are cleaned and available in the right places at the right times, getting all the required documentation and charts, and delivering patients who can't walk on their own. A number of projects therefore focused on these issues. For example, one project reduced the time for notification of a ready bed by 60 percent through better coordination and communication between various departments, and another reduced the transport time from the Emergency Department to the patient rooms by 40 percent while reducing the variation from 49 to 26 minutes.

Because Six Sigma and Lean approaches focus on reducing process variation and eliminating wasted steps, they include a considerable amount of technical rigor—data collection, statistical analysis, measurement tools, statistical process control, and more. These tools and approaches require fairly extensive up-front training for practitioners, and each project requires time to go through what is called the DMAIC cycle (define, measure, analyze, improve, and control)—a structured set of steps for applying the technical tools. In most cases, then, Six Sigma and Lean approaches take a fair amount of time. Due to the specialized technical knowledge involved, they often engage relatively few people, focusing on the direct stakeholders and managers.

Rapid Results: Breaking Logjams Quickly

Best-practices identification, process mapping, and Six Sigma and Lean tools are all logical and analytical ways of assessing and redesigning complicated processes.[8] But sometimes, analysis and logic are not enough. Old patterns can be so powerful that all the logic in the world will not lead to simplification. In those situations, a different approach might be needed—one that can break through the barriers to change and create momentum for process simplification.

For example, a number of years ago the Waterside Power Station of Consolidated Edison in New York City was having a problem with chemical spills. As one of the largest steam-producing stations in Manhattan, Waterside contained miles and miles of pipes studded with valves, pumps, and tanks filled with various kinds of chemicals and other liquids, often under pressure. In this kind of setting, spills and leaks were not only inefficient and costly, but also dangerous to workers and to the environment. The problem needed to be addressed, but the traditional approach of identifying spills, assessing root causes, developing preventive maintenance procedures, and reissuing policy manuals was not working. Leaks and spills were still occurring throughout the plant. The basic behavior of operators, maintenance workers, vendors, engineers, and the many other people working in the plant (all of whom contributed to spills and leaks) was not changed by a new procedures manual, which took months to create.

As a way of breaking this logjam, the management of Waterside commissioned a spill prevention team to examine the chemical system infrastructure in the plant and implement a strategy for reducing spills—within one hundred days. With this short-term, rapid-results objective in mind, the team set a goal of having a spill-free month in May—two months from the start date. To achieve this goal, the team selected three subprocesses that contributed to spills and leaks: delivery of chemicals, design and maintenance of valves, and maintenance of a particular chemical pumping system that was critical to plant operations. The team then asked dozens of employees, managers, and vendors who worked in these areas to contribute suggestions and solutions for eliminating spills and leaks. At the same time, the team created an overall awareness program that helped everyone understand the importance of spill prevention—and the current performance levels.

From these steps, ideas quickly emerged for reducing and preventing spills. The team reviewed the ideas as they came in and worked with the appropriate areas to implement them. Many (if not most) of the ideas were relatively modest and easy to carry out. For example, the vendors and the plant jointly purchased spill containment trays to catch overflow on deliveries; laminated cards were prepared and given to mechanics with proper torquing values for specific valves as well as correct bolt sequencing and a valve terminology diagram; a weekly walk-through of known problem valves was set up as an operating procedure of the plant. Soon the whole plant was focused on having a spill-free May—and while management was thrilled that the plant had no spills for twenty-nine out of the thirty-one days, employees and team members were actually disappointed in the three minor spills that did occur. This kind of widespread commitment to improved process outcomes helped Waterside sustain a far lower rate of spills for years thereafter.

The purpose of the rapid-results approach is to use people's natural bias toward action as a catalyst for immediate process simplification. In many situations, analysis and study can become excuses for maintaining the status quo and avoiding real process change: the "we can't do anything until we have all the data" syndrome. Moreover, when studies and analyses take a long time, conditions change so that the recommendations may no longer be on target.[9] The rapid-results approach forces the issue—giving people no choice but to figure out how the process can be simplified, accelerated, and improved in a short time—and to make adjustments as conditions change.

Rapid-results projects also invoke a bit of theater that helps get people excited and energized about process simplification. The idea of a spill-free month or the achievement of a stretch goal in one hundred days creates excitement, focus, and zest that can do a lot to overcome anxiety, cynicism, or resistance to change. In that sense, the rapid-results approach is highly engaging, not only for the team working on the process changes, but also for everyone else associated with it. With the focus on a mere one hundred days, it is clearly fast. However, a rapid-results approach usually has far less technical rigor or fewer requirements than does Six Sigma or Lean.

Work-Out: Creating a Culture of Process Simplification

Process simplification is not a onetime event.[10] Because organizations are living entities and because processes continue to evolve and create complexity, process simplification needs to be ongoing. But to take hold over time, the simplification needs to address not just work activities but also the overall social context in which work takes place, including people's motivation, attitudes, expectations, and emotions—what is often called the *culture* of an organization. The Work-Out approach was created to do just that—improve processes in the short term while shaping a culture of ongoing process simplification for the long term.

The Work-Out approach, which I've already mentioned several times in this book, was originally conceived by Jack Welch, then CEO of GE, in the late 1980s. His idea was to establish forums where large numbers of people from around the company could come together quickly to identify and make decisions about opportunities for taking unnecessary work out of the system (hence the term *Work-Out*).

In addition to eliminating unnecessary work, Welch also wanted to change the culture of GE so that process improvement and simplification would be continuous. The goal was to create an organization that would be characterized by "speed, simplicity, and self-confidence." This meant that change would happen rapidly and nimbly as business and economic conditions changed, that unnecessary steps and activities would be eliminated on an ongoing basis, and that people would have enough self-confidence to challenge the way things were done and take risks to do them differently. To foster this, the Work-Out sessions were intentionally designed to maximize the dialogue about real business problems, to provide an opportunity to develop specific and measurable solutions to the problems, and to force senior managers to make immediate decisions about these solutions. In practice this meant that a typical two-day Work-Out session might include sixty to one hundred people all focused on different aspects of a business process. After some common information sharing, small groups would then tackle different subprocesses or aspects of the problem and develop recommendations. The recommendations would then be presented to a senior manager in a "town meeting" where everyone could contribute to the dialogue, after which the manager would make a yes-or-no decision on the spot. When the answer was yes, whoever made the recommendation would then be empowered to carry it out. Figure 4-1 summarizes the Work-Out process.

FIGURE 4-1

Work-Out summary

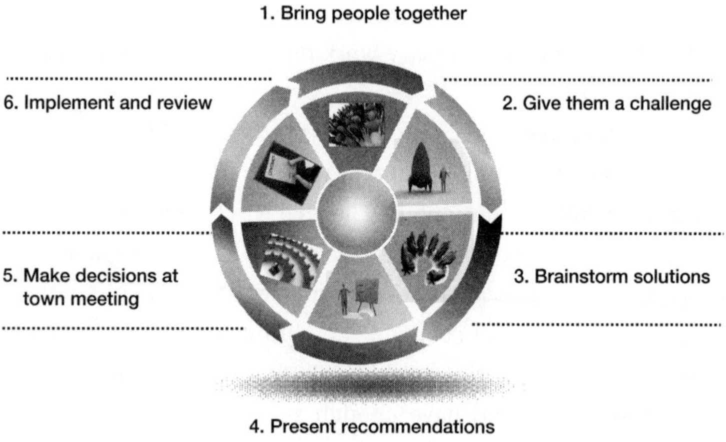

1. Bring people together

6. Implement and review

2. Give them a challenge

5. Make decisions at town meeting

3. Brainstorm solutions

4. Present recommendations

In the years since Work-Out was first developed at GE, it has been adopted and adapted by hundreds of other organizations and used extensively to simplify and improve processes of all types:

- Armstrong World Industries used Work-Out to speed up the resolution of customer claims.

- Connecticut's Department of Transportation used Work-Out to develop ideas for speeding up road repairs.

- The Ministry of Health in the African country of Eritrea conducted Work-Outs to improve implementation of its HIV-AIDS prevention and reduction strategy.

In all these cases, as well as those cited elsewhere in this book, Work-Out not only drove simplification of a specific process but also helped build a culture of continuous improvement—with more understanding of processes, greater involvement of stakeholders, and faster decision making.

Many companies have incorporated some of the other tools described in this chapter into Work-Out as a way of deepening or accelerating process simplification. For example, the results of best-practice studies can be presented at the beginning of a Work-Out session to stimulate thinking, or people from different parts of a company can use part of the Work-Out session to share and compare the way they do things. Similarly, Work-Outs can be designed according to high-level process maps, so that the different breakout groups each focus on a piece of the overall process, or process mapping can actually be done during the Work-Out event. Six Sigma and Lean tools can also be incorporated into Work-Outs to give participants additional problem-solving and analysis capabilities. Work-Outs can also be used to accelerate the progress of a Six Sigma team by bringing together stakeholders for faster problem solving and decision making after data has been collected and analyzed.[11] Finally, rapid-results projects can be commissioned as outcomes of Work-Out to make sure that the recommendations are actually implemented in one hundred days or less.

By itself, the Work-Out tool has less technical rigor than some other approaches, although these can be built in or combined. The real strength of Work-Out is its power to engage large numbers of people and foster extremely rapid—and lasting—process simplification.

Process Simplification: Connecting What, Why, and How

During the past twenty-five years, most companies have adopted the notion that processes need to be periodically redesigned and simplified—leading to widespread use of the five tools or approaches described here. While these tools and others differ in speed, the extent of technical rigor, and the degree of employee engagement (table 4-1), they all promote the notion that work can be simplified by examining processes both within and across organizational boundaries.

The key to using these tools to drive process simplification, however, is to make sure to align the what, why, and how: what processes are being addressed, why they have become overly complex, and how best to tackle them. Without matching up the answers to these three questions, it's easy to expend energy and resources on less significant processes and to try to use tools that are not appropriate for the challenge at hand.

The starting point for process simplification is thus to ask yourself what processes would give the biggest payoff if they were simplified. Look at several categories of possibilities: core operational processes central to the success of the organization; context processes that need to be done as efficiently and simply as possible

TABLE 4-1

Comparing tools for process simplification

(H=high; M=medium; L=low)

Tool	Speed	Technical rigor	Engagement of people	Comments
Best practices	M	L	M	Helps to stimulate and provoke new thinking
Process mapping	H	M	H	Makes processes visible
Six Sigma and Lean	L	H	L	Forces data-driven change
Rapid results	H	L	M	Breaks through resistance and hidden barriers
Work-Out	H	L	H	Drives process and cultural change; can incorporate other tools

but could potentially be done by service units or third-party providers; and governance processes that are critical for decision making, resource allocation, risk management, and control.

For each process selected, the next step is to ask why that process has become overly complex or ineffective. In this context, you should start with the thinking from the first part of this chapter: Do local differences need to be reconciled? Have loops and steps been added as a result of past problems that complicate the process? Would the process benefit from greater formality and rigor? Does the process need more of an end-to-end perspective to provide greater transparency and alignment across functions?

Using the answers to these questions, you can now begin to select a specific tool or approach—the how of process simplification. As noted in table 4-1, some of these tools can be applied more quickly than others; some are highly technical and may be most useful with detailed operational processes; and others are more engaging and may be most useful when processes cross many functional areas and departments.

If you go through this thought process and try to match the process, the issue, and the tool, you will boost your chances of success with ongoing process simplification.

FIVE

Curbing Complexity-Causing Behaviors

THE PRECEDING CHAPTERS HAVE DISCUSSED three major ways that managers unwittingly contribute to complexity—in how they design organizations, how they manage the product and service portfolio, and how they evolve processes for getting work done. But managers also contribute to complexity in subtler and less visible ways—in how they provide guidance, leadership, and direction for an organization. This chapter brings some of these hidden and largely unconscious personal behaviors to the surface, so that you can deal with them more effectively—and become a force for simplification in your organization.

A Tale of Two Managers

Andrea and Andre work as managers in the same company—and their behaviors illustrate how managers can make work easier or more complex for others (and for themselves). Although based on real people, the names have been changed to protect the well-meaning.

In some ways, Andrea and Andre have taken similar career paths. They are both in their mid-forties, have risen through the ranks of their consumer products firm over the past ten years, and now lead sizable divisions with responsibility for profit and losses. Andrea worked for several other companies before coming to this one, obtaining an MBA at night while also taking time out to have two children. Given all the juggling involved in her life, Andrea has become an efficient, no-nonsense manager who gives her people lots of responsibility. In contrast, Andre joined the firm directly out of an Ivy League business school, starting out in a marketing manager training program before becoming a product manager and eventually running a division of his own. He is considered a superb strategist who understands consumer trends and how to get ahead of them, and he likes to be directly involved in all the key issues facing his business.

Like most managers, both Andrea and Andre exhibit some behaviors that drive simplicity—and some that create complexity. Andrea believes strongly that individual managers should be held accountable for performance and results. She works with her people to establish clear goals for the year, as well as for each monthly reporting period. She rigorously scans the financial reports and conducts individual reviews with her direct reports to make sure that they are on top of the numbers. When problems occur, she helps identify solutions and makes sure that they are carried out. There is little wasted motion.

From the perspective of the people who work for her, Andrea keeps things simple. They all know what they need to accomplish. Everyone has a game plan to make it happen. And everyone has a scorecard and review process to know how things are doing.

Applying a mind-set developed as a track and field athlete in college, Andrea treats business like a meet. Her people compete against the competition on a public playing field with a scoreboard that records the times.

What Andrea doesn't acknowledge, however, is that her business is not always an individual performance sport. Much of the time, her business requires teamwork, collaboration, communication, and trade-offs between different objectives. In that sense, it's more like a basketball game than a track meet: players need to share the ball while performing different functions and working together as a coordinated team. Yet Andrea does little to foster team play in her organization. She does not hold regular staff meetings and in fact has little patience for meetings in general, preferring one-on-one sessions, phone calls, and e-mail. As a result, her managers often find themselves bumping into one another when their goals and priorities conflict—for example, when a number of her brand managers wound up competing with each other for the same trade spending funds. This caused not only confrontations and hard feelings but also hours of replanning and recalculation of numbers for advertising and promotion, as well as unnecessary meetings, e-mails, presentations, and general churn, at the end of which nobody was happy with the outcome.

Andre has a very different style. With his emphasis on strategic thinking, Andre feels that bringing his team together is critical so that everyone understands the overall picture and contributes to the decisions about how to move forward. He holds a quarterly off-site meeting for his team to review progress and refresh the strategic plans, and he also holds weekly staff meetings and numerous ad hoc meetings to share information and solve problems. He believes strongly in collaboration and getting everyone on the same page. This focus on alignment and teamwork means that all the people in his organization have a clear and simple framework for the division's strategic goals and a line of sight from their own work to their personal and team objectives.

What Andre doesn't realize is that his leadership style causes many of his people to feel that the strategy is a moving target and that they don't have sufficient time to actually implement it. So much time is spent sitting in meetings, analyzing data, and hearing the latest consultant study about market and consumer trends that little is left for tactical planning and execution. So while the big strategic picture is relatively clear, short-term tactical responses are iffy. Every time one of Andre's managers wants to put together a program—for example, a trade spending plan designed to promote particular brands—it's necessary to walk the ideas around to other managers, make iterative adjustments to get everyone into alignment, connect the plan to the strategy, and then present the final product to the entire team. The result is that many tactical plans get to the market late, don't work as advertised, and need to be redone.

Andrea and Andre are typical managers. Some of their leadership patterns create simplicity and make it easier for people to get results; others have exactly the opposite effect. The two managers "simplify" and "complexify" at the same time, despite having management styles that are polar opposites of each other. And if you told them that their style of leadership was causing complexity, they would be surprised, if not appalled. Neither feels like someone who adds complexity. Whatever complexity they generate is unintentional and largely unconscious.

The Complexity Blind Spot: Too Much of a Good Thing

It is curious that both Andrea and Andre, bright and well-regarded managers, are generally unaware of the complexity they create in their organization. Even more puzzling is that they each can see how the other causes complexity, but can't see the consequences of their own behavior. For example, Andrea thinks that Andre spends too much time in meetings with his people—she calls them "Kumbaya sessions and group gropes"—and has suggested to him that he be more directive with his managers. Andre, on the other hand, is convinced that Andrea is so directive that her people have to depend on her to resolve conflicts and issues; they don't have the relationships and trust needed to work things out on their own.

The reality, of course, is that both Andrea and Andre are right. We all have blind spots—things others can see but that we don't see about ourselves. Because of these blind spots, managers need feedback from others to get a more comprehensive picture of their own behavior and its consequences. This is why 360-degree feedback and a variety of associated tools have become popular and accepted as key contributors to leadership development.

Unfortunately, just giving feedback to managers is too simplistic an answer. If that's all it took, then most organizations would be paragons of simplicity and efficiency. Beyond the lack of feedback, a deeper and more subtle dynamic is at work: most managers run their organizations or their units in ways that they honestly and deeply believe are already simple, straightforward, logical, and right. They have no idea that they are unintentionally creating complexity, that they are part of the problem. Others may be to blame, but not them.

So what's going on? Two natural human tendencies keep many managers firmly on the wrong track: overdoing strengths, and avoiding areas of discomfort.

Overdoing Strengths

Robert Kaplan and Rob Kaiser, leadership consultants who have studied and worked with thousands of managers, contend that the shortcoming of most managers often is not in what they do—but in what they "over-do."[1] Managers succeed in their careers by applying certain behaviors and skills that tend to work for them, both in their personal lives and in business. With the reinforcement of success in mind, they continue these behaviors and build on them when moving into new or more responsible positions. Over time, a manager can become reliant on these behaviors as a core skill set so that when things become difficult or challenging, the manager engages in these behaviors more and more, since this is what has worked in the past. The problem is that in many cases, doing more of the same doesn't get the same results. It's like putting more and more hot pepper into a pot of stew—at some point, it becomes inedible.

This dynamic helps to explain Andrea and Andre. Andrea always had success in the past with individual goal-setting and an emphasis on individual accountability. In her current position, however, she overdoes the focus on individual performance, which causes her to underemphasize team alignment. Andre does just the opposite. He overdoes team building and collaboration, which causes him to unintentionally underemphasize individual performance and initiative.

Avoiding Areas of Discomfort

Further exacerbating this lopsidedness is the natural anxiety that most people have about doing things outside their comfort zone. Andrea is comfortable in one-on-one settings but is less skillful about working in groups and teams. As a result, she gravitates to individual work and unconsciously avoids team situations. Andre, of course, does the opposite. And then both of them rationalize their choice by calling it "the best way to get things done."

All managers—in fact, all human beings—unconsciously and unintentionally avoid doing things that make them anxious or uncomfortable, and instead fill their time with activities that they know how to do and that make them feel competent. Children avoid homework, college students avoid writing papers, and managers avoid difficult performance reviews. And all of them say that they are too busy or don't have enough time to do these anxiety-provoking and difficult things.

Consider the following question. Imagine that your CEO asks you to take on a special one-day-a-week assignment working directly with her. It involves interesting travel and some exciting work—but requires you to do the rest of your job in the remaining time. Would you take the assignment? I've asked this question of thousands of managers over the years, and 99 percent of them say they would take the assignment and figure out a way to do their regular jobs more efficiently. And in discussing why, they acknowledge that at least 20 percent of their time is regularly taken up with things that keep them busy and comfortable, but that don't add much value.[2]

The Double Whammy

From a psychological standpoint, then, most managers—like Andrea and Andre—overdo their strengths and simultaneously avoid the areas that make them uncomfortable and anxious—areas that are often the opposite of the managers' strengths. This is the dirty little secret of management inefficiency and a major source of complexity in organizations. It's not logical and rational, and it's often difficult to uncover and discuss. But it's there and at work nonetheless.

What is ironic is that the typical feedback to Andre and Andrea—and many managers like them—actually does them a disservice. Most feedback, even the best-designed 360-degree surveys, tends to focus on strengths and weaknesses, with the assumption that managers should build on their strengths and rectify their weaknesses. So in this case, Andre would be told that team building was a strength that he should do even more of, and that he should work on how to develop more individual accountability. But the message he should be getting is that he is overdoing the team aspects of leadership and that he should dial back on team building, which would then make it easier for him to drive individual goals and accountability. As Kaplan notes, feedback should be more about calibrating the dial on a continuum of behavioral choices (in this case, from team focus to individual focus) rather than an absolute focus on strengths and weaknesses.[3]

Much of the managerially generated complexity in organizations comes from overdone behaviors—from too much of a good thing and the associated avoidance of its opposite. This dynamic is difficult to see because managers tend to think they are doing the right thing in the right way. But too much of one right thing, coupled with too little of its opposite, is often wrong.

Leadership Behaviors That Cause Complexity: Unintentional Upsets

Managerial behavior tends to create complexity in three common leadership areas—strategy and planning, goal setting, and follow-up and communications. For each area listed in this section, ask yourself if you are giving it too much attention or too little and if you are indulging in the associated complicating behaviors. You can then consolidate your answers on the questionnaire presented in table 5-1.

Strategy, Planning, and Budgeting: How Much Detail Is Enough?

Developing an organization's strategy and then translating the strategy into operational and financial terms is one of the most critical leadership tasks—whether at the corporate, divisional, departmental, or functional level. Every organization has some sort of process to do this in a coordinated way (hopefully a simple and straightforward one). No matter what the process requires,

TABLE 5-1

How much complexity am I causing?

For each of the managerial behaviors listed here, place an X in the column for the frequency that applies to you. For the behaviors that you do most often, make some notes about how they foster complexity in your organization. Then at the end of the questionnaire, select one or two areas in which you would like to experiment with new behaviors that would increase simplicity. For those behaviors that you do fairly often or all the time, what are the implications for fostering complexity? What specific opportunities do you have to make shifts that would drive simplicity?

Strategy, planning, and budgeting	Hardly ever	Occasionally	Fairly often	All the time
1. Seeking the perfect strategy	❐	❐	❐	❐
2. Delegating strategy to others	❐	❐	❐	❐
3. Overdoing top-down direction	❐	❐	❐	❐
4. Overdoing bottom-up freedom	❐	❐	❐	❐
5. Allowing the planning cycle to run on and on	❐	❐	❐	❐

Goal setting and demand making				
6. Backing away from expectations	❐	❐	❐	❐
7. Engaging in charades	❐	❐	❐	❐
8. Accepting seesaw trades	❐	❐	❐	❐
9. Setting vague or distant goals	❐	❐	❐	❐
10. Not establishing consequences	❐	❐	❐	❐
11. Setting too many goals	❐	❐	❐	❐
12. Allowing deflection to preparations and studies	❐	❐	❐	❐

TABLE 5-1 (*continued*)

	Hardly ever	Occasionally	Fairly often	All the time
13. Misplacing demands on staff and consultants	❏	❏	❏	❏
14. Setting arbitrary goals without dialogue and buy-in	❏	❏	❏	❏
15. Micromanaging	❏	❏	❏	❏
16. Indulging in laissez-faire management	❏	❏	❏	❏
17. Being unclear about roles and responsibilities	❏	❏	❏	❏
18. Having weak work-planning disciplines	❏	❏	❏	❏

Communications	Hardly ever	Occasionally	Fairly often	All the time
19. Not asking for feedback	❏	❏	❏	❏
20. Producing overcomplicated presentations	❏	❏	❏	❏
21. Mismanaging meetings	❏	❏	❏	❏
22. Drowning the world in e-mail	❏	❏	❏	❏

however, managers can create or reduce complexity in the way that they carry it out.

Here are five of the most common complexity-creating managerial behaviors in the planning and budgeting arena. I've observed them often in the course of working with hundreds of companies over the years. Ask yourself if you've been doing any of these:

1. Seeking the perfect strategy

2. Delegating strategy to others

3. Overdoing top-down direction

4. Overdoing bottom-up freedom

5. Allowing the planning cycle to run on and on

The Quest for the Perfect Strategy

Most everyone acknowledges that strategy formulation is not easy. It requires understanding of the marketplace, recognition of trends, careful financial analysis, competitive scanning, customer sensitivity, technological predictions, and assessment of your own capabilities. All these data points then need to be mixed together with a dash of creativity to come up with a compelling and realistic strategy.

Given the vast array of potential inputs and the sophistication required to put them all together intelligently, some managers spend countless hours combing through the data, commissioning additional studies, analyzing reports, conducting planning meetings, and generally trying to create the perfect strategy. But just as few chefs can create the perfect soufflé, so too can very few (if any) managers create the perfect strategy. There will always be more data, more analysis, and more opportunities, and the world will keep changing. At some point, managers need to take what they've got, draw conclusions, and move their teams into action. As McGill professor Henry Mintzberg has pointed out, strategy needs to be crafted iteratively over time rather than finalized.[4] Overdoing data collection and analysis—and avoiding commitment to a few key action-implications—can create enormous churn and complexity.

The Willingness to Let George Do It

Because strategic planning can be so daunting, some managers avoid the process entirely and delegate it to others—to planning functions, to professors, or to consultants. While this can also lead to the quest for the perfect strategy, the bigger danger from delegating strategy is that it can then become disconnected from the commitment and capability of the organization and thus becomes unlikely to be implemented. Early in my consulting career, I remember sitting in a manager's office while he described a challenging strategic problem. After an hour of discussion about different approaches, I noticed a series of colored binders on his shelf and asked him what they were. "Those are the various consultant and in-house strategic studies we've done on this problem," he replied. Turning over the strategic planning to others might reduce a manager's discomfort about coming up with the one right answer, but it often creates complexity by proposing solutions that nobody except the consultant really understands or buys into.

The Certainty That Father Knows Best

Effective strategic planning and budgeting usually requires a balance between top-down direction and bottom-up input. Some managers create complexity by overdoing direction from the top. They rightly believe that managers at lower levels and in other functions need to be given strategic parameters and financial guidance—but these same higher managers don't want to bother with iterative dialogue with people about what it will take to achieve the numbers and whether the numbers are realistic. In the absence of that dialogue, subordinate managers may put together plans that have little chance of being realized, which leads to frantic makeup actions later in the year. A manager in one company calls these elements of his annual plan the "go-get-'ems"—the gaps or bogeys that are put in the plan with no clear path for how they will be accomplished.

The Freedom to Do It Right or Do It Over

Managers also fall into the opposite trap by providing too much leeway at lower levels to develop plans and budgets, without

guidance about what is acceptable and required. In these cases, the upper-level manager may want the plan to be developed from the bottom so that there is real commitment and a realistic picture of what will be accomplished. More often than not, after lower-level managers have done huge amounts of work to produce these plans, someone adds up the numbers and finds, to everyone's dismay, that they fall short. Then the word goes out that everyone needs to revise his or her plans to plug the gap between the submitted plans and what's needed to satisfy shareholders. These recycles of the planning process create enormous churn and added complexity.

The Planning Cycle That Never Ends

The final way that managers unintentionally add complexity to the planning and budgeting cycle is by having insufficient discipline in regard to timing and finalization of outputs. Often this is exacerbated by other dynamics. Too much or too little direction, for example, may lead to multiple cycles. In other cases, managers simply hesitate to put a stake in the ground for timing, not wanting to rush their people or force shoddy work or make them take time away from other things. But by being considerate of everything else going on and not putting discipline around the process, managers are in fact adding to the overall time and churn and complexity. As one manager said, "We start the planning cycle around midyear, and finish it around midyear of the next year."

Do you recognize any of these managerial behaviors in yourself? If so, make a note of them on the questionnaire in table 5-1.

Goal Setting and Demand Making: Poor Calibration Creates Complexity

Once strategies and budgets are created (no matter how much complexity is involved), managers need to translate them into specific goals for departments, units, teams, and individuals—and then make sure that people actually carry them out. This fundamental loop—setting goals and seeing that they are carried out—is a prime source of complexity in most organizations.

The irony is that most managers know the right way to set goals and make assignments, but somehow they just don't do things that way. They know that goals should be aligned with the overall strategy, should be measurable, should provide "stretch" (to stimulate innovation and learning), but should also be achievable. Managers also know it's important to hold people accountable for goals, ask for work plans and timetables, conduct reviews, and make sure that rewards and consequences are associated with getting to the finish line. Anyone who has been through Management 101 or read any of a thousand business texts knows the basic drill. Yet most managers, despite all their knowledge of the right way to set and achieve goals, unconsciously ignore or avoid actually carrying out many of these behaviors. Stanford Business School professors Jeffrey Pfeffer and Robert Sutton call this discrepancy between what managers know they should do and how they actually act the "knowing-doing gap."[5]

The inability to set solid, clear goals and follow up on them to ensure that they're met creates enormous churn and complexity in organizations. Imagine if the crew of a rowing team all put their oars in the water at different times and pulled in different directions. Instead of moving forward, the boat would rock, splash, and turn in circles; the crew members would not only lack a sense of accomplishment, but also grow angry and frustrated with each other. Without effective goal setting and follow-up, organizations also flounder around instead of moving in a purposeful direction.

My colleague Robert Schaffer noted many years ago that the ability to make demands on other people was one of the most universally underdeveloped management skills.[6] He explains it from a psychological perspective. All people—including managers—have a basic human desire to be liked. When they need to challenge other people to step up and achieve more, managers often unconsciously fear that any number of uncomfortable reactions will cause them to be less well liked or perceived—for example, that the person will argue with the goal ("Gee, Boss, it's way too tough"); that the person will resent being told what to do ("Who does she think she is?"); that the person will prove that the goal doesn't make sense ("Hey, Boss, I don't think you've seen the most recent data"); or that the person will accept the goal but not really own it ("I'll do it if you say so"). The manager also may fear that if the subordinate takes on the goal and then doesn't meet the target, it might lead to an uncomfortable confrontation about performance. "Then what?" the manager muses. "Do I have to fire the guy, or reduce his bonus, or get into an argument?" Given all these scenarios, it's easier to not press people too hard. They'll like you better that way—and you won't have to put yourself in an uncomfortable situation.

The paradox of this unconscious logic is that most people actually like being challenged or stretched. They see it as a way of affirming that the boss believes in their ability. In fact, research shows that the most exciting and energizing times in most managers' careers—and the times they cite as the most developmentally valuable—are when they are asked to do something that stretches them beyond what they themselves thought they could do.[7] In practice, much of the hesitation that managers exhibit about making demands is based on their own anxiety, rather than on reality.

Seven Deadly Sins of Demand Making

Robert Schaffer has identified what he calls "the seven deadly sins of demand making": traps that managers fall into, all of which cause complexity in organizations. As you read the descriptions, ask yourself if you recognize any of them in your own work, and then add them to your responses to the questionnaire in table 5-1.

1. *Back away from expectations:* One way to avoid the discomfort of demand making is to backpedal away from specific, short-term requirements. At that point, what sounds like a goal really becomes a wish that people can choose to ignore. Example: "We really need to cut expenses but OK, budget for level expenses year over year; but I'd sure like to see some reductions when we get into the new year."

2. *Engage in charades:* You can also avoid demands by letting your subordinates know that you're not really serious about getting to the goal—that it's just an exercise or a dance that you have to do for appearances' sake, but you know it's not really going to happen. Example: "Look, I don't know where we're going to get a 15 percent increase in sales, but I had to put it in my budget, so you've got to put it in yours."

3. *Accept seesaw trades:* It reduces the pressure of demand making if you allow your people to make trade-offs in their goals—so that if they take on one goal, they'll get relief on another. Instead of holding firm and saying that both goals have to be achieved, the manager will cave in and accept an either-or approach. Example: "Sure, we can increase sales, but you know that we'll have to give deeper discounts to do it."

4. *Set vague or distant goals:* Another way to avoid making real demands is to water down the goals by not having clear measurements or by putting the time frame far out into the future. This is the equivalent of telling your people to give it the good old college try rather than holding their feet to the fire with specifics that have to start right now.

Example: "By this time next year, I want to see a significant improvement in staff utilization in your department."

5. *Don't establish consequences:* The next avoidance mechanism is to not really hold people accountable for their commitments, so it's impossible to differentiate between those who achieve goals and those who do not. Example: "Even though you didn't reach your targets, I know that you tried hard, so I'm going to give you the same bonus as everyone else this year."

6. *Set too many goals:* Another common demand-making sin is to give people a bushel basket of goals, far more than they could possibly achieve. This then allows them to pick and choose the goals that they either want to do or find easiest to do—but not necessarily the ones that are most important from the organizational or strategic perspective. Example: "You'll see on the screen the thirty key goals I want everyone in the division to concentrate on this year."

7. *Allow deflection to preparations and studies:* The final sin is to avoid setting tough goals without more data, more studies, more analysis—overdoing any number of preparatory activities that delay the moment of commitment to a real goal. Example: "If you really want to reduce inventory, the first thing we have to do is commission a study to find out who caused the stuff to be ordered, why it's not getting used as scheduled, and whether we need to rethink our whole inventory control philosophy."

Other Complexifying Ploys

In addition to these sins of demand making, I've seen six other managerial behaviors create complexity in regard to goals and demands. Ask yourself if you've been doing any of these things, and again note your answers on table 5-1.

- Misplacing demands on staff and consultants

- Setting arbitrary goals without dialogue and buy-in

- Micromanaging

- Indulging in laissez-faire management

- Being unclear about roles and responsibilities

- Having poor work-planning discipline

Misplaced Demands.   A recurring but invisible source of complexity in organizations is the tendency of many managers to establish ambitious goals and convey tough demands to people who do not have the authority to get them done, such as functional staff and external consultants. Because of the anxiety associated with making tough demands, managers often find it easier to use surrogates to convey their expectations instead of confronting their subordinates directly. This allows them to feel that they are doing the right thing about setting goals in concise, measurable, and time-bound ways—but without having to deal with the consequences of disagreement or inability to respond. It's like sending a messenger to convey bad news. Unfortunately, just as in the ancient world, messengers bearing unwelcome messages often get slaughtered. And in the corporate world, this means that staff and consultants often are ignored or pushed back on, which creates additional cycles of work, misunderstandings, hard feelings, and general frustration.

Consider the following case: The chief operations officer (COO) of a diversified manufacturing conglomerate was concerned about rising inventory levels. To deal with the situation, she called in the vice president of supply chain, whose department was made up of staff experts in procurement, logistics, warehousing, and distribution—and read him the riot act. In no uncertain terms, she made it clear that it was his job to get inventory down by 15 percent in the next three months (even though inventories were owned and managed by the businesses). The supply chain vice president, happy to have a mandate from the top, then sent a team of his people out to each of the business divisions of the company to work with them to get their inventory down to the required levels. In each location, however, the staff people got a different story about why inventory was above planned levels, and why no further action was necessary at this point. In one site, for example, a new product had been introduced ahead of time, which had increased inventories; in another location, the business unit had increased inventories to gear up for an upcoming product promotion. After weeks of meetings and studies, the vice president went back to the COO and was forced to report that inventories were still on the rise and that no plans were in place to reduce them.

This convoluted and complexity-creating process of placing tough demands on staff and consultants instead of on line management—the "demands triangle"—is illustrated in figure 5-1. The simple alternative, eliminating all the unnecessary work, is for the manager to place demands directly on line management—and then have the staff people provide help and support. That, of course, requires tough demand making, so it's rarely done.

Arbitrary Goals.   Another managerial behavior that causes complexity is handing out targets without discussing what the targets mean, how they are to be achieved, and what parameters need to be followed. The familiar dynamic often occurs when the manager knows what the organization needs to accomplish and understands what needs to be included in an effective goal, but is anxious

FIGURE 5-1

The demands triangle

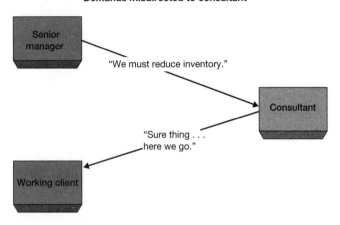

Demands misdirected to consultant

Senior manager

"We must reduce inventory."

Consultant

"Sure thing . . . here we go."

Working client

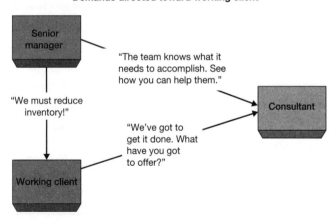

Demands directed toward working client

Senior manager

"The team knows what it needs to accomplish. See how you can help them."

"We must reduce inventory!"

Consultant

"We've got to get it done. What have you got to offer?"

Working client

Sources: Adapted from Robert Schaffer, "Make Sure the Client Makes Demands," *Journal of Management Consulting 1* (Fall 1982); and Robert Schaffer, *High-Impact Consulting*, 2nd ed. (San Francisco: Jossey-Bass, 2002), 187–192.

about questions that might be raised or resistance to the goal. Consequently, the manager just issues the goals and avoids the dialogue.

Micromanagement. A recurring challenge for most managers is to find the right balance between what Kaplan and Kaiser call "forceful leadership" and "enabling leadership."[8] When a manager overdoes the forcefulness, the tendency is to stay involved at a detailed level instead of giving subordinates the leeway to get things done on their own, in their own way. Sometimes this pattern stems from the manager's feeling of being the only one who knows how to get the job done right, making it necessary to provide detailed direction. In other cases, particularly at senior levels, managers get more anxious the further away they get from the day-to-day action and may compensate by wanting more frequent reports, reviews, check-ins, and data. This helps them feel that they have a hand firmly on the helm of the ship.

Unfortunately, micromanagement often has the opposite effect from what practitioners intend. It reduces the empowerment and vitality of people who actually have to get things done and reduces their ability to make decisions and take fast action. It also reduces their ability to develop broader skills and abilities, so that the organization ends up being dependent on the micromanager, who may even become a bottleneck for decision making. At the same time, micromanaging also may lead to complexity through the creation of additional reports, reviews, and meetings. At the most senior levels, an entire infrastructure can sometimes be created to feed data and information upward so that it is available at all times.

For example, several years ago the CEO of one of the largest consumer products companies in the world held detailed monthly reviews with each of his division presidents and key function leaders. In preparation, each senior executive, with the help of an army of finance people, put together a review package that included sales, marketing, and cost data broken down into dozens of specific categories. The executives had to be ready to answer questions about everything in the package. Many hundreds of people were involved in this monthly effort, which consumed thousands of hours. Since it was mandated from the top, however, few people publicly questioned the value of all this work. When a new CEO was appointed, one of his first actions was to shift the business reviews to a quarterly schedule and to focus on exceptions. The business didn't miss a beat—and thousands of hours of work were eliminated overnight.

Laissez-Faire Management.   The opposite end of the spectrum involves overdoing the enabling side of the continuum and creating complexity through insufficient direction. Many managers who have been schooled in team-based approaches and the value of empowerment hesitate to give people too much direction. They assume that once they give a subordinate clear and challenging goals, they just need to get out of the way and let the person figure out what to do. But again, it's a matter of balance. If a manager gives out an assignment and then waits months to see what the team comes up with, the chances of going off course are fairly high—and later correction requires a lot more effort than it would have taken to stay on the right track in the first place.

For example, a food and beverage company was introducing a new product that had the potential to be a blockbuster. Five flavors were tested with consumers—four of which did very well, while one was rated as subpar. However, the team members had told pilot retailers that five flavors would be available, so they kept moving forward with the variation that consumers didn't like. The head of the consumer foods business, who had empowered the team to do whatever was necessary to get the new product on the shelf, now heard that everything was on track for the launch date, and so he didn't review the details of how the team was proceeding. It was only by chance that he found out about the disappointing flavor—which would have turned off consumers and compromised the entire launch—and was able to pull the plug on it at the last minute. But in the meantime, huge amounts of effort had been wasted on something that should have been corrected much earlier.

Unclear Roles and Responsibilities.   Another source of complexity in the goal-setting and follow-up area is failure to clarify who is responsible for tasks and decisions—and who is not responsible. In most organizations, projects and processes require coordination and collaboration across many functions or departments—and ambiguity about who makes decisions, who has veto power, and who needs to be involved can create enormous churn, misunderstanding, and rework.

A common tool or framework used to sort this out is called a RACI chart—which is a simple way of setting out who has responsibility, who has ultimate accountability, who needs to be consulted, and who needs to be informed. Completing this chart requires dialogue with the various stakeholders to find out who has each of the roles—and to build sufficient trust that all those involved will stick with the bargain and not try to usurp each other's roles. For example, in a complicated acquisition integration project, one of the key work streams involved the rationalization of benefits across several sites. In the first weeks after the deal was announced, no one knew whether the business, the local HR group, the finance function, or the regional HR "comp and benefits" unit would lead the rationalization, and who would have the ultimate call. Each group scrambled to collect data and identify alternative scenarios, specifying the benefits that could be changed, the cost and morale implications, and the timing for various announcements. After it became clear that the four parties were not only doing redundant work but also tripping over each other and sending mixed signals to employees, the CEO brought them together for a RACI discussion. It was determined that the local HR group would chair the project (responsibility); that the head of the business would make the final decision about what to do (accountability); and that both finance and the HR regional group would be consulted (consultants). Once this was clarified, the project proceeded much more smoothly.

Poor Work-Planning Discipline. The final complexifying behavior under discussion is a lack of basic disciplines for turning goals into detailed work plans. Managers often find it surprisingly hard to undertake the necessary steps for realizing their goals: identifying key tasks, specifying who is accountable for each task, agreeing on a timetable for starting and completing tasks, designing measures to assess progress, and building in reviews of progress to make midcourse corrections. The problem is that these disciplines often seem so mundane and unexciting that managers don't pay them much attention—assuming either that the steps to get things done are obvious or that lower-level managers will take care of the details.[9]

A number of years ago, I was sitting in a meeting with key managers of a manufacturing site. They were planning a plant expansion and spent several hours going through the various steps needed for constructing the physical site, moving machinery, hiring additional workers, shifting work flows, and other key tasks. The discussion was lively and everyone was engaged, with dozens of pages of flip charts covering the walls. At the end of the meeting, the managers took their pages and their individual notes and walked out, agreeing to meet in two weeks to review progress. I then asked the plant manager if anyone was going to write up the overall plan and make sure that everyone agreed on the next steps and timing. He reassured me, saying that everyone on his team knew what he or she needed to do and that there was no need for any additional "bureaucracy." When the team met two weeks later, he was surprised that several tasks had fallen through the cracks because everyone thought someone else was taking care of them, while other tasks had been done by more than one person, and everyone was confused about the overall timing.

If you recognize any of these managerial behaviors as your own, make a note of them on the questionnaire in table 5-1.

Communications: Unconscious Breeding Ground for Complexity

A good part of the managerial job involves communicating plans, directions, progress, and other information to members and stakeholders of the organization. Effective communication in essence creates a central nervous system that allows an organization to get work done; poor communication creates enormous complexity as signals are blocked, misunderstood, or misdirected. But managers rarely recognize their own complicity in making communications complex, as it's easier and more comfortable to attribute communications problems to other managers, to employees' inability to grasp the point, to HR, or to the communications function for not getting the right messages out there.

On the off chance that you may be unintentionally creating complexity through poor communications, ask yourself if you've succumbed to any of these behaviors:

- Not asking for feedback

- Producing overcomplicated presentations

- Mismanaging meetings

- Drowning the world in e-mail

Feedback? What Feedback?

Some people have a knack for conveying even the most complex messages in clear, straightforward language, sometimes using analogies or pictures or diagrams. Other people can take a simple idea and make it virtually incomprehensible. The problem is that often we don't fully recognize where our own work falls on this continuum, especially when subordinates, colleagues, or customers don't want to admit that they didn't really understand something; or don't want to embarrass a senior, powerful person by saying that the message was confusing. These kinds of communications missteps can have profound consequences for managers and organizations, leading people to make erroneous assumptions or take misguided actions. As professors David Collis and Michael Rukstad point out, "most executives cannot articulate the objective, scope, and advantage of their business in a simple statement," and this shortcoming severely compromises the company's ability to execute on the executives' strategy.[10]

The challenge for many managers is to have the discipline, and the courage, to regularly ask for feedback about their communications—to find out quickly whether the right message is getting across in the right way. Without this feedback loop, it is too easy for people to walk away with different ideas about what to do, leading to wasted motion and uncoordinated activity. Whether you are talking with someone one-on-one, meeting with a group, or speaking at a town-hall meeting or webcast, you can build a request for feedback into the end of your message. With individuals, you can simply ask them to summarize the key points that they heard; in a group, you can ask a few people to do the same; and with a presentation, you can ask for written feedback or have a few volunteers speak out. The key is to ask for feedback rather than happily assume that the message you are trying to convey is the one that is being heard.

Death by PowerPoint

Mark Twain once apologized for writing a long letter, saying that he didn't have time to make it shorter. The same applies to presentations in organizations. When presentations are long and complicated, it is often a signal or symptom of the presenter's not having taken the time to highlight the key points in a way that everyone can understand quickly.

Since the advent of Microsoft's PowerPoint and other desktop graphics tools, presentations have become ubiquitous in organizations and a core method for conveying ideas, recommendations, and proposals. When used properly, these presentations can be very powerful ways of communicating. Well-done slides can focus the issues, present data clearly and quickly, and foster constructive dialogue. That's the good news. The bad news is that many managers either don't quite know how to use the tool or unintentionally abuse it. So instead of clear and simple communication, presentations too often become reports masquerading as slides, or cuteness competitions, or ways of preventing instead of facilitating dialogue. In fact, creating long, overloaded PowerPoint decks has become an industry in itself, taught and reinforced in business schools and outsourced by consulting firms to experts in India who crank out data-loaded templates on a 24/7 basis. The result in many cases is what managers refer to as "death by PowerPoint"—presentations so long and complex that they bore their audience senseless.

To counter this trend, one firm instituted the "one-minute drill" for presentations—forcing people to reduce their message to its essence, in slides that could be presented in only a minute.

Mangled Meetings

Meetings are not just a fact of life in organizations; they're a way of life. Some managers can spend up to 80 percent of their time in meetings, particularly in organizations that are heavily matrixed, global, and process focused. Unfortunately, as most managers will attest, much of the time spent in meetings is unproductive, frustrating, and wasteful. So instead of being a source of simplicity—to get everyone quickly on the same page—meetings are often a source of complexity, with people walking out feeling confused, or unclear about what happens next, or without a decision about an issue.

The irony, of course, is that most managers know exactly what's needed to make meetings productive drivers of increased simplicity. Effective meeting management is one of the most popular management development topics, with courses offered by every management training firm and most internal training departments. Hundreds of articles and books have been written about the subject. John Cleese of Monty Python fame even put out a training video on the topic: *Meetings, Bloody Meetings.*[11] All these inputs say more or less the same things: clarify the purpose of the meeting and what needs to be accomplished; get the right people (and only those people) in the room; differentiate between sharing information, problem solving, and decision making; have a designated leader and facilitator; create an agenda and time schedule in advance; manage the interactions; watch the time; spell out the next steps. Yet how many managers actually run meetings with these disciplines?

In reality, many meetings in organizations are at least partially ritual get-togethers that meet people's psychological needs for social interaction and the sharing of accountability. Most managers, even at very senior levels, do not want to feel that they are running the enterprise by themselves or doing their work in isolation; they want to share the burden and the excitement with colleagues. That is why, despite all the training and knowledge about effective meeting management, most attendees collude with meeting leaders to water down the disciplines they all know. The challenge for simplicity is to reduce at least some of this unproductive meeting churn to either give people more time or make the meetings more valuable.

For example, in GlaxoSmithKline's pharmaceutical research organization, the creation of very large, cross-functional drug development teams had spawned numerous meetings of teams and subteams—so many that some researchers were spending more time in meeting rooms than in labs. When Amber Salzman became head of development operations, she sponsored a "fit for purpose" initiative that required all team leaders to redesign their team memberships and their meetings and tailor them only to the issues required for that stage of drug development. That initiative saved thousands of hours of professional time and refocused many of the teams on what was most important for bringing their products to market.

A different approach was instituted at The World Bank some years ago. As a way of making people aware of the expense of meetings, a device was installed in a number of well-used meeting rooms. The instrument automatically calculated the cost of the meeting by multiplying the number of people in the room by an average employee hourly rate and by the length of the meeting. This knowledge alone led to a significant reduction in meetings and meeting duration.

Lapses of E-Mail Etiquette

E-mail might seem insignificant or innocuous, but inbox overload is a serious source of organizational complexity. This is despite the previously unimaginable communications capacity engendered by e-mail and wireless technologies. Who would have thought twenty years ago that it would be possible to communicate almost instantaneously with virtually anyone around the world at any time, at very little cost? The problem is that the new capabilities have come without instruction manuals about how to make them work effectively—and the unfortunate result in too many cases is added complexity instead of simplicity.

For instance, when a manager sends large numbers of people a message on issues that many of them don't need to know about, it just burdens colleagues with low-value information that distracts them from matters more important. A frequent culprit is the "reply all" button, which can create hundreds of e-mails, often about insignificant topics such as meeting schedules. Another source of complexity is the recirculation of documents ("attachments") in multiple drafts and redrafts. This creates extra work for the recipients, who must read and organize the material, particularly if they must comply with document retention (and destruction) standards. Worse, recipients can become confused about which version is the most current and make edits or comments on the wrong one—a waste of time and a source of errors.

Again, ask yourself if you recognize any of the communications-related behaviors in your own work. Note your answers on the questionnaire presented earlier in table 5-1.

What's a Manager to Do? How to Become Conscious About Unconscious Behaviors

If you've read this far—and thoughtfully considered the twenty-two specific behaviors described in this chapter—you now realize that you may be a prime source of complexity in your organization. But if these managerial behaviors and others like them are largely unconscious and driven by psychological factors, how can they be overcome? Do managers need to undergo years of psychotherapy to be cured of complexity-causing neuroses and to get the balance right between "overdoing" and "underdoing" leadership activities?

To make it simple, the answer is no. Therapy is not a precondition for simplicity. But that doesn't mean that changing behaviors and rooting out unintentional complexity-causing actions is easy. It takes a real commitment to simplicity, hard work, self-examination, and experimentation—and a support system of colleagues who can help. In many ways, rooting out complexity-causing behaviors is similar to attending Alcoholics Anonymous or other twelve-step addiction-reduction programs. You have to admit that you cause complexity and then have a support group that can reinforce your desire to change.

Changing Leadership Behaviors at The World Bank

Here's a case study in which an entire senior management team worked to change its individual and collective behavior.

When James D. Wolfensohn became president of The World Bank in 1995, he initiated a whirlwind series of changes meant to change the bank's mission and overcome doubters who were saying "fifty years is enough" for this multinational institution.[12] As part of this effort, Wolfensohn refocused the bank away from large infrastructure lending (such as dams and bridges) and more toward poverty alleviation through social programs, health, and education. This shift in mission also entailed new organizational structures—fewer layers and networks of technical specialists; new lending and technical assistance products; and processes that were more streamlined for making loans, tracking projects, and managing the administrative infrastructure.

The combination of so many changes on multiple fronts would have been daunting and intimidating for almost anyone, but The World Bank's leadership team found it especially challenging. Generally trained as economists and technical specialists and not as general managers, the bank's executives had never faced such a total transformation. Suddenly they found themselves in new positions, with restructured organizations, and expected to work in dramatically different ways. Most of them were willing to help transform the bank, but they often fell back on their traditional behavior patterns, which tended to be bureaucratic, slow, internally focused, and control oriented.

By 1998, the result was gridlock. Dozens of strategic initiatives were under way, but few were making progress; managers were inundated with messages and reports that they couldn't absorb and were being pulled into endless meetings that never seemed to reach conclusions or decisions. Wolfensohn was frustrated, feeling that many of the managers were dragging their feet. And many of the managers felt that the only time they could get anything done was when they were away from the bank on missions to client countries, which gave them even less time to get things done back at the Washington headquarters.

Realizing that the situation was largely related to their own leadership, managing directors Sven Sandstrom, Caio Koch-Weser, and Shengman Zhang (Wolfensohn's key lieutenants at the time) initiated a focused process for changing managerial behavior, starting with themselves and the top twenty-five vice presidents who reported to them. To launch the effort, the managing directors sent a note to all the vice presidents, asking them to identify ways that they could be more effective both individually and collectively. Each manager (including the managing directors) then was assigned a coach (either an external or internal consultant) to help with this thinking. The role of the coaches was largely to hold up a mirror so that the managers could each reflect on their own way of managing, both through individual discussions and by getting input from people who worked with them.

The individual managerial work immediately began to create new patterns. Sandstrom and Koch-Weser, for example, realized that they were trying to oversee and track dozens of projects without a clear sense of priorities and without a governance rhythm. In response, they worked with a team to inventory all of the major "change projects" going on in the bank, separate the ones that were internally focused from those that were externally focused, and then list the top five or six priority projects in each category. They then set up a pattern of scheduled reviews for the priority projects so that people would know what they had to report on and when the report was due. The vice presidents also identified personal issues, ranging from how they used their time to how they communicated with their people.

In addition to the individual changes, the managers identified a number of things that they could do collectively to work more simply and effectively. One very powerful idea, for example, was to coordinate their collective travel schedules. Since the managing directors and vice presidents had responsibility for projects around the world, many of the executives were constantly on trips to developing countries or to visit with donor governments or other aid agencies. As a result, the extended management team—the top twenty-five or so managers—rarely if ever wound up in the same place at the same time. Meetings and reviews often had to be repeated with different groups of people, and other meetings were ineffective because key people were missing and unable to call in. To counter this constant motion and simplify the overall governance of the bank, the top executives all agreed to spend one common week each month in Washington and to schedule key internal meetings for that week. This eventually led to the concept of a "corporate day" each month for Wolfensohn and the top management team to review key initiatives, solve problems together, and share what they were learning from various projects.

While this introspection and experimentation was going on, Wolfensohn also worked with an external coach to see whether any of his patterns were adding to complexity and could be changed. Although he was the originator and energizer of the bank's transformation, he wondered whether any of his own behaviors were inhibiting or delaying progress. In exploring this question, he came to realize that the way he was structuring his own time was sometimes making him a bottleneck for decisions. As a result, he added a senior assistant to better coordinate and focus the many demands on his time, reorganized his personal staff, and coordinated his travel schedule more closely with the rest of the managers. He also encouraged his managing directors to work with him as a team rather than just as individuals. This allowed him to focus more on the external parts of his role with the confidence that the team would manage the internal affairs of the bank.

This process of reflection, dialogue, experimentation, and simplification continued over the next couple of years—including sessions in which the management team shared their learning with each other—leading to the evolution of significantly different ways that Wolfensohn and his team managed the bank. The logjam that had slowed down the implementation of strategic initiatives was broken, and by the time Wolfensohn retired in 2004, the institution had been totally transformed.

How You Can Make It Happen

As The World Bank case illustrates, rooting out managerial behaviors that cause complexity can have a profound impact on organizational health and success. But you don't need to wait for a total, comprehensive, corporate program to get started. Here are a few steps that you can take right now to drive simplicity in your own leadership role:

1. Fill out the questionnaire in table 5-1, and use it to reflect on your own behavior. Ask yourself whether you recognize any of the behaviors described in this chapter in your own work, and think about their implications for fostering unnecessary complexity.

2. Share your questionnaire results and thinking with a few other managers or colleagues who know you well.

Depending on the nature of your relationship, this could be your boss, a team of people who report to you, peers, or friends. If you want total confidentiality, hire an outside coach or consultant. Make sure that you pick people who will be honest and straightforward with you—and give you real feedback. Our own views of ourselves often need to be challenged or at least supplemented with a perspective from others.

3. From your own reflection and the feedback from colleagues or a coach, select one or two specific ways that you can experiment with making things simpler by changing your own behavior. These don't need to be huge changes—start small and gain some confidence. For example, try to change your e-mail patterns or the way that you plan and run meetings. Once you have some success, share what you've done with your colleagues or coach and identify additional simplification opportunities.

4. If possible, recruit others to go through the same process of reflection, experimentation, and learning—and meet with them as a group to share progress and ideas. Building a support group for changing behaviors can be a powerful way of reinforcing your own attempts to change while helping others do the same. Eventually, you may see common patterns that are based on your organization's culture—and that might be better attacked collectively.

5. Finally, if you are in a position to drive simplification on a broader basis in your company, you can insist that your management team go through the process of reflection, experimentation, and learning together. You might also engage your HR function to help facilitate the dialogue and

eventually build the expectation of managerial simplification into your company's performance management and rewards process.

A Never-Ending Quest

While the steps described here are simple, they are definitely not easy. Looking at yourself in a mirror is a difficult and challenging task, especially when you open yourself to seeing things that you might not like. But if you really want to drive simplification in your organization, it's not enough to just change the structure, the products, and the processes. You may also need to change yourself—not once, but over and over again.

SIX

Strategy for Simplicity

CONSIDERED SEPARATELY, THE FOUR SOURCES of complexity—structure, products, processes, and management behavior—can all be attacked with various tools and approaches. But sometimes the real task is to put these tools and approaches together to wage a comprehensive war on complexity and create an ongoing culture of simplification and productivity. That's the focus of this chapter—how to weave the available tools into an integrated and sustainable strategy for simplification.

To begin, consider General Electric, a company that has used simplification as a driver of productivity for more than twenty years.[1]

Building Simplicity into the Culture of GE

By rights, managing GE should be one of the most complex operations on the face of the earth—after all, GE's businesses range from broadcasting to financial services to locomotive manufacturing, and it has hundreds of thousands of employees, tens of thousands of managers, and thousands of locations around the world. Yet perhaps because of its inherent complexity, GE has made simplicity a key component of its operating system and a major source of productivity improvement year after year. Simplicity at GE is more than just a slogan or a value or a principle—it's a way of thinking and an inherent part of the culture.

For example, in reviewing so many industries and markets around the world, GE's strategic planning and budgeting activities could easily tie the company in knots. To prevent this, GE's senior managers constantly take stock of the planning and budgeting processes and fine-tune them as the company evolves. As a case in point, CEO Jeffrey Immelt realized in 2003 that the strategic planning process was becoming redundant with the budgeting process. The two were calling for much the same data, but for different time frames. To prevent unnecessary and repetitive work (which cascades to thousands of people in such a huge company), Immelt reframed the strategic planning process so that it was squarely and simply focused on growth; he renamed it the "growth playbook" and made sure it came with straightforward instructions about what needed to be included (and what did not). The budgeting process then flowed naturally out of the growth plans with far less confusion. At the same time, the message that growth was the primary focus for strategic planning was hammered home.

In addition to fine-tuning the process to keep it simple, Immelt and his management team also work hard to present the company's overall strategy in a way that most people can understand. Figure 6-1 portrays the strategy as it appeared in the 2007 annual report and letter to shareholders. The key here is that each GE business and subbusiness could take this diagram and use it as the starting point for developing its own plans—with high-level financial targets, key business principles, and core strategic opportunities for

FIGURE 6-1

GE's strategic principles

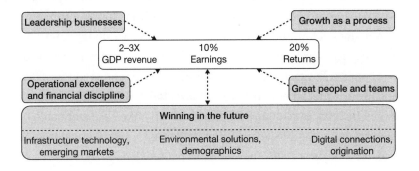

Source: GE Annual Report, 2007, p. 9.

future growth. It allowed everyone at this huge and highly diverse company to have a common framework and language for moving forward.

To keep the process organized and therefore simple to deal with, GE establishes a strict calendar for its planning and budgeting (and other key governance mechanisms) so that managers across the entire enterprise know what they need to submit, to whom, and by when. This prevents the effort from dragging out for large portions of the year. And finally, when GE managers present their plans and budgets, they learn how to capture the key messages succinctly, simply, and clearly in relatively few pages with bullet points and what are called at GE "takeaway boxes" with summary statements. As Susan Peters, GE's chief learning officer, notes, "Pitches here are an art form . . . It's important both what and how you present. You need to know your stuff and it has to be crisp. The complexity and sheer size of GE forces simplicity: there are so many issues and industries and countries to cover that we've got to cut through it."

Simplifying what would be an otherwise highly complex planning process, of course, does not guaranty that every business and every strategy within GE will achieve its objectives, especially when markets collapse or unforeseen external forces intervene. But it does allow the senior leadership team to understand and identify risks earlier and make faster decisions about what needs to be changed. For example, when the suddenly frozen credit markets and worldwide recession severely affected GE Capital's business model in 2008, Immelt and GE Capital head Mike Neal were able to restructure and reposition GE Capital within *weeks*—an enormous task for a business with thousands of people divided into dozens of business units around the world.

The Evolution of Simplicity at GE

All this emphasis on simplicity at GE didn't happen by chance. It began in the early 1980s, when then-CEO Jack Welch challenged each of his managers to make their business number one or two in its industry—or they would have to "fix, sell, or close" it.[2] This straightforward (but very difficult) imperative not only triggered an ongoing simplification of the GE portfolio, but also drove simplification of the company's structure at both the corporate and the business unit levels. At the time, many of GE's businesses were actually holding companies with dozens of separate business units, each with a profit-and-loss (P&L) statement of its own. To become top players in their industries, the businesses needed to consolidate their separate units to give them enough mass to compete. For example, the lighting business had units for incandescent lamps, fluorescent lamps, halogens, lighting systems, international business, and others. To achieve top industry status, GE combined these units into one integrated business with strong centralized functions (manufacturing, engineering, sales, marketing, finance, human resources) that served all the product groups. Pulling the units together this way also eliminated a tremendous amount of cost. On top of that, groups of GE businesses had been clustered into "sectors," with sector executives and staffs. Welch quickly eliminated the "sector" level, feeling that it added little extra value, and had the dozen or so major business leaders report to him directly.

By the end of the 1980s, Welch had achieved his goal of having each business be number one or number two in its market—and had simultaneously simplified the structure of the company. Hundreds of separate units were now consolidated into thirteen major businesses. In the process, sectors were eliminated, lower-performing businesses such as consumer appliances had been sold, higher-performing businesses such as NBC had been bought, and huge amounts of excess cost had been eliminated (representing almost 100,000 fewer jobs).

Simplicity as a Way of Life

Welch realized, however, that this was just the beginning. As he put it, he had changed the hardware but not the software of the company. Although the structure was simplified, people were still doing their work in the old ways. It was taking too long to make decisions, and most employees were not engaged in figuring out how to improve the company. To take the company to the next stage, Welch initiated the Work-Out process, as described in chapter 4. However, the goal of Work-Out was not just to "take work out" of the system, as important as that was, but also to create a culture that was explicitly characterized by "speed, simplicity, and self-confidence." Thus, each of the hundreds of Work-Out sessions in the early 1990s was more than just a vehicle for eliminating bureaucracy and streamlining processes; it was a tutorial on the new mind-set, reinforcing the behaviors of speed, simplicity, and self-confidence with the GE managers and employees who participated and who eventually numbered well into the hundreds of thousands.

This massive cultural reeducation process at GE in the first half of the 1990s was reinforced by various other key initiatives that were in addition to and complemented Work-Out. One initiative focused on learning best practices from other companies, particularly in different industries, and then quickly incorporating them into GE. Another taught process-mapping skills to all GE managers and then integrated these skills into the Work-Out sessions. A third taught managers a framework for accelerating change, which became known as CAP (change-acceleration process). Finally, each business was required to de-layer so that it had no more than eight management levels. All this, of course, was in the context of delivering quarterly and yearly business results. In fact, every initiative was positioned as an enabler for achieving business results and not as a "nice to do" or optional activity.

GE's Crotonville Leadership Development Center served as a central coordination point for these initiatives and incorporated the key messages into all of its other training. At the same time, GE's HR organization explicitly revised the performance management and promotion criteria and processes to match the new expectations for managers, including the mind-set of simplification. And Welch was explicit and public about his reasons for rewarding some senior managers and firing others on the basis of the new criteria.[3]

As a result of this combination of approaches, GE's management corps was completely transformed between approximately 1989 and 1994. Speed, simplicity, and self-confidence went from an interesting aspiration to a day-to-day expectation. For the most part, managers who didn't buy into this way of thinking had either self-selected themselves out of the company or been replaced.

In the mid-1990s, an even more rigorous approach to simplicity was introduced: Six Sigma training. Every manager in the company was required to complete the training and successfully accomplish a green belt process-improvement project. And to put teeth into this, bonuses and promotions were tied to these expectations. This not only ratcheted up the capability of GE managers to drive process improvement and simplification, but also gave them a common language for working with each other on these issues.

When Jeff Immelt became CEO of GE in 2001, he added an external "growth perspective" to the cultural foundation that had been created over the past two decades. Without changing the basic notions of simplification and continuous improvement, he made sure that they were directed outward, toward customers. He felt that if the company was going to grow as rapidly as necessary, it would need to form more intimate partnerships with customers to anticipate their needs and design solutions with them. For example, as Mark Begor, CEO of GE Money Americas, noted, "Although we got a lot of customer input previously, we were too internally focused, probably spending 75 percent of our time on internal issues. We've flipped that in the last few years and given much more influence to our client teams versus our operational process teams. In fact our client teams live with our customers and are co-located there."

Simplicity Through Continuous Improvement

The net result of these initiatives is that simplicity is built into the GE culture and way of thinking. While it is reinforced and refreshed through Crotonville courses and additional corporate or business unit programs, it is essentially passed on from manager to manager with the understanding that it is a requirement for survival and success. Lloyd Trotter, a former vice chairman of GE, describes the thought process like this: "We teach managers that they need to start with the 'answer,' which is that their business needs double-digit earnings improvement every quarter and every year. They quickly realize that sales growth without leverage won't do it. So they have to figure out how to drive growth while increasing productivity. We don't complicate it: Material comes in the front door and products go out the back door. We have to get rid of any waste in the middle while also figuring out how to have the products or services be more valuable for our customers."

Embedded in this simple statement is the underlying expectation that all GE managers need to constantly reach higher levels of performance. As Mark Begor notes, "We don't celebrate well `. . . [A]fter we achieve something, we feel good about it for a few minutes, then ask, 'What didn't go as well as it should have?' and then we raise the bar for the next project." As a result, successful managers at GE are always looking for new ways to get their jobs done, new ways to run their businesses, or new businesses that they should run. Begor, for example, leads a business that has reinvented itself several times. It started as a consumer credit company, then became a company that provided branded credit cards, then was a marketing and sales vehicle for retailers, and now is a company that offers a variety of branded credit products through retailers. He says that GE does best when managers create a crisis that forces people to rethink their assumptions, root out waste, and figure out new ways to do things. "There's no finish line at GE," he says.

Susan Peters, the chief learning officer, notes that GE is deeply rooted in having a process culture—which means that managers constantly look for streamlining and simplification opportunities. She is in charge of Session C, for example, the yearly talent assessment and planning process for GE. As she describes it:

> Previously it was very paper intensive, with huge confidential books about people in each business. I remember spending long periods of time at Kinko's making duplicate pages myself that had to be done secretly out of the office so no one would see them. Now we've changed all that with technology. Everything is digital—the ratings, the definitions, the courses, the

forms. Just click to add or change something. Everything is on the digital tool. So now we don't have to take hard copies to meetings; we look at a screen together or view it online.

Teaching Simplicity—One Manager at a Time

The striking thing about GE is that the drive for simplicity is so widespread—across businesses, industries, continents, and national cultures. Over time it has become a self-replicating part of the company's DNA. To some extent it clearly starts at the top. Senior leaders have all modeled the focus on a very small number of clear and simple priorities—whether the priority is "make your business number one or number two" or "growth." As these simple messages cascade through the organization, the managers each translate them into one or two simple and focused priorities that they expect their teams to accomplish. As Susan Peters says, "Prioritization and focus are keys to doing well. Sure, there are other things that are not on the priority list, but you do them differently or more slowly."

This emphasis on simplicity and focus is conveyed not only through modeling but also through active mentoring. GE managers are teachers who have brutally candid conversations with each other and with their people. Issues get on the table without a lot of politicking or whitewashing, and they go up to higher levels without filtering. And for the most part, the question is not "Who is to blame?" but "What do we need to do?" This behavior is taught and reinforced over and over again. Lloyd Trotter tells this story:

> I walked into a meeting and the manager who was presenting
> had forty slides that he planned to cover in half an hour. Instead
> of wasting everyone's time, I called for a quick coffee break and
> helped that manager pick out five charts that would provide the

basis for a good discussion and a decision. I didn't berate him or embarrass him for doing a tree-chopping exercise. I understand that people are nervous presenting to senior executives. But at the end of the day, it was important for this manager to learn how to be self-confident enough to distill the issues down to the salient facts and the actions we need to take.

This doesn't mean that everyone makes it at GE. Many people don't connect to the culture and can't master the pace, the energy, the continual raising of the bar, the candor, and the need to focus and simplify. They are counseled out of the company, or let go, or self-select themselves out. But the core group of managers who do get it pull others along and orient the newcomers so that the culture becomes self-sustaining.

Simple Is Never Easy

Despite more than two decades of simplification and a powerful culture of results through simplicity, GE still struggles with complexity. It's a never-ending battle. At the portfolio level, the senior executive team is constantly culling out businesses that no longer have sufficient growth potential, even if they were star performers in the past. The external analyst community is constantly pushing for even more transparency and simplicity for understanding GE's various businesses, how they fit together, and how they generate synergistic results. And inside the company, GE still struggles with mechanisms for gluing the company together across its businesses and functions. The current approach is to create "councils" for functions and for commercial operations—but managers who run these councils also have full-time "day jobs" in their businesses and are constantly on guard against "council overload."

GE also faces ongoing challenges with managing layers and levels—as the company gets bigger and more global, layers tend to increase. In addition, as the prevailing culture gets stronger and more solidified, managers tend to hire people who think like the managers themselves, and groups thus become less open to new ways of thinking.

But GE managers are aware of these issues and challenges and tend to face them head-on—not perfectly, not easily, but forthrightly and with a continuous focus on results. And in so doing, they demonstrate how simplicity can make a profound difference in a complex world.

But What If You're Not GE?

The evolution of simplicity at GE is an impressive story. But not every company has the resources, talent, and time that GE brought to bear. GE invested millions of dollars in Work-Out, Six Sigma, and its myriad other simplicity programs and initiatives. And while the return on that investment was many multiples of the expense, few companies can afford the up-front cost. Nor do most firms have CEOs and boards with the vision, faith, and patience to create a multidecade (or even a multiyear) transformation, and with the courage to deal with the resistance, criticism, pain, and struggle of implementing fundamental organizational and cultural change.

All this is good to have, but it's not essential. Here's a look at another company that has transformed itself, its results, and its fundamental nature through a focus on simplification: SEB, a Stockholm-based financial services organization serving both retail and commercial customers in northern Europe.[4] Founded in 1856 as the first commercial bank in Sweden, the bank merged in 1972 with a major Swedish retail bank. In the three decades that followed, SEB made dozens of acquisitions, essentially becoming a holding company with banks and life insurance operations in ten countries, representative offices around the world, and more than twenty thousand employees. But expanding its scope and geographic reach left SEB with a high cost base compared with its peers and relatively weak capitalization—both of which were serious obstacles to achieving sustainable profit growth. That was the situation that faced Annika Falkengren, a seventeen-year veteran of the bank, when she became CEO of SEB in the fall of 2005.

Determined to make SEB the leading bank in northern Europe, Falkengren quickly realized that complexity was perhaps her greatest enemy. The acquisition and holding company strategy had left SEB with multiple brands and systems platforms, along with thousands of IT applications, product variations, governance structures, HR systems, and financial reports. To grow, the bank needed to be transformed into an integrated operating company. Thus Falkengren's first move was to initiate what she called the Road to Excellence, which called for a two-year concentration on achieving operational efficiency. This phase was then to be followed by focused growth in selected areas of strength—with the understanding that a business area had to first earn its right to grow.

To operationalize this concept, Falkengren established ambitious financial targets in areas of sustainable profit growth, return on equity, and rating quality, as well as a longer-term goal of being number one in selected business segments and markets. She then reorganized the bank into four customer segments: merchant banking, retail (including Sweden, Germany, and the Baltic countries along with the bank's card operations), wealth management (including both asset management and private banking), and life insurance. Across the segments, the support functions (IT, operations, HR, finance, marketing, communications, legal) were all centralized and charged with developing "one function and one solution" that would drive consistency, simplicity, and cost reduction. The overall theme was to build one bank—emphasized by the company's term *One*

SEB—with increased cross-selling and improved cost-synergies in which knowledge and expertise were leveraged throughout the bank for the clear benefit of the customers.

Once the new structure was in place, Falkengren and her team then began to engage employees in specific simplification and improvement projects. Since SEB people had such different line-ages, languages, and national cultures, however, they had no common way of addressing change. In response, Falkengren and her team created an operational excellence program called the SEB Way to create a common culture, a common language, and other tools for continuous improvement. In 2006, the first year of the program, 40 percent of the company's staff went through SEB Way sessions, out of which were launched 180 transformation projects across all areas of the company. Many of these were focused on cost reduction, systems rationalization, and creating common functional practices, while others were aimed at product simplification. For example, several product families in retail banking (such as consumer loans and savings accounts) were reformulated to be more understandable and accessible to customers, and then were branded under a common moniker: *simplified.*

To reinforce a culture of continuous improvement, Falkengren and her team incorporated much more tightly SEB's core values of "commitment, mutual respect, professionalism, and continuity" into the training and communications. Falkengren herself spent a lot of time on internal communication, addressing what and how the bank was moving forward. This dual focus on P&L results *and* behaviors—the extent to which an individual contributed to One SEB—was then built into the performance review process. Managers were assessed, rewarded, and promoted not only on whether they achieved results but also on the extent to which they acted in accord with the SEB Way.

By the end of 2008, the equivalent of 7 percent of the workforce had been freed up through the SEB Way—resources that were reinvested in sales activities and other aspects of the business. Despite substantial write-downs and difficulties in the capital markets, SEB still posted an operating profit (although lower than 2007) and higher overall income and business activity. By no means was the bank's transformation complete, but a foundation built upon simplicity had been created.

Putting It All Together: Strategy for Simplicity

So what do GE's decades of simplification, SEB's twenty-first-century transformation, and the experience of the many other organizations I've cited have to teach? How can a manager create an integrated architecture of simplicity that can accelerate the achievement of results, make it easier for people to get things done, and create more powerful and sustaining connections with customers?

Although every organization needs to shape its own strategy, five steps should always be considered, generally in this sequence:

1. *Declare:* Position simplicity as a driver and enabler of business results.

2. *Restructure:* Simplify the organization's structure (using some of the tools and approaches described in chapter 2).

3. *Achieve:* Capture early business results through process streamlining or product simplification (using some of the tools and approaches described in chapters 3 and 4).

4. *Sustain:* Develop sustained momentum by building capacity and incentive for simplification into the culture of the company (referring to some of the behaviors described in chapter 5).

5. *Repeat:* Learn from experience, and create additional and continuing waves of simplification.

This strategy is summarized in figure 6-2, and each element is then described in more detail below.

Declare

The starting point for an integrated simplification strategy is to explicitly make the connection between simplicity and business results. This step is critical for making sure that simplification is not just a value, slogan, or feel-good theme. If you want simplification to make a difference for your organization, the bottom line is that it needs to hit the bottom line: make it a business imperative.

Both GE and SEB clearly position simplicity as a business imperative. At GE, simplicity is a pervasive, overarching principle

FIGURE 6-2

Strategy for simplicity

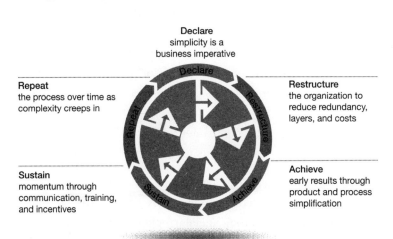

Declare
simplicity is a
business imperative

Repeat
the process over time as
complexity creeps in

Restructure
the organization to
reduce redundancy,
layers, and costs

Sustain
momentum through
communication, training,
and incentives

Achieve
early results through
product and process
simplification

that managers are expected to use as a way of continually improving their business results. It shows up in GE's model for operational excellence, in its growth traits, and as a key theme in its yearly Session C talent assessment. Ever since Welch's focus on "speed, simplicity, and self-confidence" in the early 1990s, simplicity has been a lens through which GE managers view their businesses. SEB's focus on simplicity is, of course, more recent, but it's just as clear. When Annika Falkengren became CEO, she immediately stressed the importance of creating One SEB as the key to becoming the leading financial services institution in northern Europe. Doing that required extensive simplification of organizational structure, IT applications, governance mechanisms, product variations, and go-to-market strategies—as well as a common leadership approach. There was no mistaking that simplification was a business issue.

ConAgra Foods, described in chapter 1, is another example of simplification as a business imperative. Gary Rodkin made it clear to his managers and associates as soon as he took the reins in 2005 that the company's complexity was driving up costs, cutting into profit margins, and hindering investment in growth opportunities. He set specific cost-reduction targets that were clearly tied to eliminating duplication, and he publicly declared simplicity, accountability, and collaboration to be key priorities—ones that would constitute 50 percent of the performance review criteria for managers.

Here are a few other companies whose senior executives have positioned simplicity as a key business driver:

- *Siemens:* When Peter Loscher became CEO in 2007, he set out to simplify an overly complicated structure that might have contributed to financial irregularities. He quickly declared that creating a streamlined, transparent structure and a less complex product portfolio were two of his early priorities for turning around the business.

- *Nielsen:* After consumer ratings and research company Nielsen was taken private by a consortium of equity firms in 2006, new CEO David Calhoun focused the company on becoming "open, integrated, and simple" as the strategy for improving operating performance and developing tighter, more collaborative relationships with customers.

- *L'Oréal USA:* The company had grown via a business model in which each division was somewhat autonomous, and in 2008, U.S. CEO Laurent Attal determined that simplification would need to be a key goal for taking L'Oréal USA to the next stage of growth and profitability, especially in light of an economic downturn and rising materials costs. He then focused his team on becoming a "beauty company without boundaries" in which simplification was a key strategy.

Of course, declaring simplicity as a business imperative is only a first step, and it means very little if not followed up with actions and results. But not positioning simplicity in a business context means that people won't take simplicity seriously, won't make it a priority, or won't be able to translate simplification into specific business goals.

Restructure

Once it is clear that simplicity is a business imperative, the next step is to move into action fast—and the most visible and dramatic simplification steps are usually connected with organizational design. Although it is certainly possible to start with product or process simplification (depending on organizational needs), restructuring does more to stir the pot and break old patterns. In essence, if you want to drive change across an organization, you need a bit of theater, drama, and energy.

Both GE and SEB began their simplification journeys with dramatic restructuring efforts. GE consolidated smaller units into major businesses that were required to become number one or number two in their various markets. In addition, Welch eliminated sectors and forced each business to prune layers. These steps triggered large-scale simplification of the entire GE structure. SEB began with the consolidation of all the functional staff groups into enterprise-wide units that had to develop single, common solutions for the four newly created business segments. This, too, represented a major simplification of the company's structure.

In both cases, however, structural simplification was not driven just for its own sake or for making a statement about simplification. Structural simplicity at both GE and SEB generated significant bottom-line results, both in terms of cost reduction and in terms of the ability to serve customers more quickly and effectively. Structural simplification also sharpened accountability, making it clear who was on the hook to produce results and who needed to make things happen. In addition, savings from structural simplification were invested back into product and process improvements and were also used to help fund change programs and education efforts to support a broader focus on simplification.

ConAgra Foods also started with structural simplification. As described earlier in the book, CEO Rodkin's first major move was to shift from semi-autonomous branded food businesses to an integrated operating structure. This led to the creation of enterprise-wide functional groups (similar to the ones at SEB) that supported snacks, dairy, grocery, frozen, and commercial "food groups." This shift produced immediate and significant cost reductions while also establishing the foundation for further simplification.

As anyone who has been through reorganization knows, organizational restructuring can be painful and distracting. I am not recommending shaking things up and creating chaos as a precursor to simplification—that would be disruptive and counterproductive. The idea is to quickly identify real structural opportunities for simplification where results can be achieved and the power of simplification can be demonstrated relatively quickly. With GE, SEB, and ConAgra, the opportunities were at an enterprise level and therefore involved everyone. But that's not always the case. For example, at L'Oréal USA, one of the first opportunities for simplification was to consolidate the creative resources that supported the luxury brands group. Previously, each brand had its own team for dealing with ad agencies, managing packaging, and doing collateral and marketing materials. This created extra cost and process inconsistency. It also meant that major customers were dealing with multiple L'Oréal people for activities such as counter design for department stores. By pulling all its ad-oriented people together in one group, under one manager, L'Oréal USA reduced costs, simplified processes, and streamlined customer relationships all at the same time. But it also sent a signal to the company that simplification was a serious and important priority—since the possession of brand-level creative teams was a very long-standing tradition that was now being broken.

Achieve

Once you've made it clear that simplification is a business imperative and taken steps to simplify the organization structure, you can start dealing with product and process complexity. It's similar to childhood development—start first with the gross motor skills involved in restructuring and consolidation, and then develop the finer motor skills required to simplify products and processes.

As mentioned earlier, this is not to say that you cannot focus on product rationalization or process streamlining before changing the organizational structure—and for some organizations, that will make sense. In most cases, however, first doing some amount of structural cleanup makes it easier to focus on products and processes, for two reasons. First, restructuring is often perceived as a wake-up call, a shock to the system that forces people to reexamine the way they do things. Second, after restructuring, people need to reconfigure their processes and ways of working—it's impossible to keep doing things in the same way if the structure is not there to support it.

The key in any case is to generate early and substantial business results through product or process simplification, or both. The choice of starting point really depends on your situation and where the most significant opportunities lie. If you need to do a quick diagnosis or assessment of opportunities, that might be useful—as long as you don't get caught up in a long process of study and analysis to find the perfect starting point. If you are like most managers, you have a pretty good sense of where opportunities might exist, and you can tap into your colleagues and associates who probably also have ideas. You also probably know already where processes might be broken—where things take too long or cost too much to accomplish. And you probably know which products are not producing as much value as the rest, either for you or for your customers. Any of these insights can suggest useful places to start.

As described earlier in the book, many tools and approaches will help you drive product or process simplification. Your company may already have some of these tools available, and if need be, you can hire external expertise to help you with some initial pilot tests. As you get started, you should think about getting early results from your efforts—and about building internal capacity to use the tools more extensively and continuously. Make sure that you are not just catching fish but teaching your people how to keep fishing over time.

As noted earlier, when GE shook up and simplified its structure through the 1980s, it wound up with 100,000 fewer people and a fundamentally different pattern of organization. Because of the structural shifts, people couldn't continue working the way they had done previously. As Welch noted, "We had taken out the people, but not eliminated the work they were doing." Thus it was a natural evolution to focus on process simplification—through taking work out—as the next phase of the process.

SEB also began its simplification efforts with a major structural change—the shift to bankwide functions to support the business segments. This created the context for the process-simplification efforts called the SEB Way—workshops designed to create common processes for these new enterprise functions. Simultaneously, SEB also simplified its product offerings. Its leaders realized that they couldn't offer all products to all markets and hope to support these offerings in a cost-effective way. So, for example, the leaders focused on merchant banking in Norway and pulled out of the life insurance business there; and in several other Nordic countries, they got out of retail banking and concentrated on private banking. While these shifts created some difficult publicity, they were necessary steps for achieving product focus.

ConAgra Foods also moved on from structural change to product and process streamlining. After reorganizing the company into four groups supported by enterprise functions, CEO Rodkin culled the product portfolio, selling off lower-performing brands such as meats and cheeses. He also initiated a large-scale process-simplification effort, aiming to consolidate and simplify the basic processes necessary for running the company.

These early product- and process-simplification efforts all share two key elements. First, they produce measurable and important results—not just studies, recommendations, reports, or systems. In this way, simplification comes alive—it is not a theoretical construct but a business initiative that makes a difference. It produces savings or revenues to reinvest, which convinces people that simplification is worthwhile. Second, these initial efforts engage and touch many people, rather than being confined to a few senior executives. Ultimately, simplification is a sport that requires everyone to be in the game and not sitting on the sidelines, and involvement needs to begin early on, as it did at GE, SEB, and ConAgra Foods, or it will never become part of the culture.

Sustain

By positioning simplification as a business imperative, making rapid structural changes, getting early results from process and product streamlining, and engaging large numbers of employees, companies can build up a head of steam. The challenge then is to sustain this momentum beyond the initial adrenaline rush so as to build simplification into the culture and fabric of the organization. To do this, companies can use communications, training, and HR systems.

Communications to Sustain Momentum

Strategic communications can reinforce the message that simplicity is important, that it's a business imperative, and that it can indeed make a difference. For simplification to take hold, senior executives need to become simplicity evangelists. They have to preach and teach—not as moralists but as change leaders, and not occasionally but all the time, as part of every business message. Simplicity needs to be a drumbeat, constantly and consistently reinforced in personal interactions, written materials, town meetings, speeches, and business meetings.

But that doesn't mean that the message is conveyed only as a formula or with rote and overused phrases. Managers must apply the concept of simplicity to real, day-to-day issues, making simplicity come alive in the moment. Lloyd Trotter's earlier vignette of helping a GE manager cull down a forty-slide presentation deck is a good example of in-the-moment teaching. Annika Falkengren from SEB also notes that much of her time is spent communicating about simplicity and transformation, building it into every interaction as well as every formal speech and meeting. For example, she often tells her people: "Think about the client first. Does the client want to pay for us to do the same things in different ways in different places?" Gary Rodkin and his senior team take a similar approach at ConAgra, constantly refocusing people on the importance of simplicity and how to use it as a lens for solving the current business issue. A manager at The World Bank once said to me that the key to effective change in a large organization was "one thousand cups of tea"—meaning that key messages had to be internalized by each person, one at a time, through individual interaction.

In addition to communicating about simplicity, managers also need to make their messages about other business topics simple. It's not enough to say that simplicity matters; managers also need to communicate everything simply. Obviously, this doesn't happen overnight—communicating simply and clearly takes skills that may need to be refined over many years. But senior managers in particular need to get this started and establish the expectation that simple and clear communication is to be expected. One of the early tests, for example, is whether your company's or division's strategy can be explained by your managers (and subsequently by everyone else) in one or two sentences. This may take hard work—to boil down complex ideas into simple pictures and statements. But it is critical for making simplicity more than a slogan. This also may be the place where structured approaches, such as the one-minute drill for slide presentations, may be appropriate.

Training to Sustain Momentum

It might sound obvious, but simplification won't happen if everyone approaches it differently. You need to create a common framework and language for simplification, and then train everyone on it. This not only gets everyone on the same page, but also creates widespread capacity for action and multiplication of results.

All the companies discussed in this chapter went down this path. GE, of course, is well known for developing structured simplification approaches such as Work-Out, CAP, and Six Sigma. Critical to the success of these programs, however, was their central orchestration: they all emphasized the same basic principles and tools, whether they were applied in a financial services business, a manufacturing plant, or a sales team. They were tailored to accommodate the differences of local business needs, but the overall framework was the same everywhere. The same could be said for the SEB Way and ConAgra's RoadMap.

In addition to being orchestrated from the center, these training efforts had several other features that turn out to be critical for sustaining simplification over time:

- *They propelled people into action to produce real results.* While they included certain amounts of conceptual material, the true aim of these efforts was to apply simplification concepts to current business problems—so that everyone who participated was not just "educated," but also transformed into a change agent.

- *They deliberately aimed at producing measurable change in a few months or less.* In essence, the idea was to keep it simple: pick off a process or a product issue that could be addressed and resolved quickly as a way of building momentum and reinforcing the change effort. If the problem or topic was large and complex, then the training helped people to break it down into something simpler that could be handled right away.

- *They were rolled out quickly across the whole company and run largely by in-house people.* To do this, external consultants or experts were used to help design the materials and run the pilot tests or initial sessions, but internal resources were trained as soon as possible to drive the broader-scale rollout. At GE, every business designated some internal Work-Out consultants who worked alongside the external consultants for the first round of pilots—and then took more and more of the lead as the process expanded. SEB also trained internal "challengers" to run the SEB Way workshops, and ConAgra developed a team of transformation leaders who could work with the business units to design RoadMap sessions, as well as dozens of facilitators who could support the transformation leaders.

- *They were so interactive as to be mind-bending.* Training can't just convey concepts and teach tools; it also needs to shape mind-sets and influence behavior. The tools the trainers and facilitators bring to the table are just a beginning; the truly critical role of training is to stimulate dialogue, encourage people to question assumptions, create a safe space for employees to come up with their own simplification solutions, and give each other feedback on the kinds of behaviors that inadvertently breed complexity in organizations (such as those described in chapter 5).

Incentive Systems to Sustain Momentum

People tend to do what they are measured on, and to continue to do what they are rewarded for. Someone who drives simplification and is not somehow rewarded or recognized for this achievement is unlikely to pay much attention to other opportunities to cut wasted motion. Conversely, if simplification is consistently rewarded—publicly and transparently—rewards or other recognition can provide a powerful incentive for further simplification, both by those who benefit directly and by those who see what behavior pays off. So to lock in simplification for the long term, you need to align the human resource systems with the actions you want people to perform.

This equation sounds simple and logical on the surface. Tell people what you want, and reward them for doing it, or punish them for not doing it. In that sense, most people in organizations are little different from the lab animals that continue certain behavior if they are rewarded with food pellets and that avoid other behavior if they receive electric shocks. In reality, however, organizational performance and reward systems are usually not so straightforward; they encompass multiple goals, measures that don't always reflect real behavior, and incentives that are not always directly linked to either the measure or the goals. The result is the confused and counterproductive practice that my colleague Steve Kerr refers to as "rewarding A while asking for B."[5]

GE is a good illustration of how HR systems and incentives can reinforce and sustain the behaviors required for simplification. When Jack Welch first introduced his speed, simplicity, and self-confidence mantra, many people wondered what this really meant and how seriously it needed to be treated. Eventually, however, some businesses crafted lists of managerial attributes associated with each of the three themes. Some businesses even constructed 360-degree questionnaires that would give managers feedback about how well they exemplified these attributes. Other businesses organized workshops, and still others used the attributes at management meetings. After a year or so, the corporate HR team consolidated and sharpened the attributes and built them into a new set of official GE "leadership behaviors" that GE managers should strive toward.

While all this activity was interesting and instructive, the leadership behaviors didn't become real drivers of change until they were publicly and dramatically used as the basis for high-level promotion decisions. At an annual officers' meeting, Welch announced that he had asked two of his business leaders to leave the company, despite their having achieved their financial targets, because these managers did not measure up on the leadership attributes. He then explained his thinking through a two-by-two matrix with "results achieved" on one axis and "leadership behaviors" on the other (figure 6-3). The essence of his explanation was that achieving financial results was no longer enough—managers were now expected to achieve their results while behaving in accord with the tenets of speed, simplicity, and self-confidence. That was the one sure path to promotion. Falling short on both was a clear route out of the company, and falling short on either meant trouble, even though results had always been paramount at GE.

This was a stunning announcement, and it changed everything. Most people had assumed that managers who achieved results were off the hook in terms of the behaviors. After Welch's action, leadership behaviors were no longer "nice things to strive for"; now they were requirements for succeeding at GE, along with the achievement of results. They had real teeth and were now officially part of the performance management process.

The bottom line is that sustained behavior change doesn't happen by itself. If you want people to behave differently and to build simplification (or any other behavior) into your company's culture, then you need to pull all three levers: communicate clearly what is

FIGURE 6-3

GE performance matrix

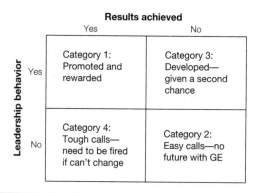

expected, train and develop managers to meet those expectations, and then reward (or punish) people accordingly.

And then, of course, you need to start all over again, which brings me to the last step in the overall simplification strategy.

Repeat

As the examples demonstrate, simplicity is an ongoing journey and not a destination. The currents of complexity run unabated and need to be dammed and diverted again and again. Moreover, even if you have successfully built simplification approaches and behaviors into the culture of your organization, they need to be periodically refreshed, renewed, and revised as new employees, managers, and leaders take the stage, and new business challenges come to the forefront. If you are serious about simplification, you need to be prepared to keep at it, over and over, for as long as your organization exists.

GE's focus on simplification for almost thirty years is perhaps the best illustration of this persistence. As GE's Mark Begor explains, "These investments over the decades have created the building blocks of our culture such as speed, customer-focus, and simplicity." But even at GE, it's never over. As chief learning officer Susan Peters notes, "No company is as simple as it used to be ten years ago, and that's true for GE, too. The pace of information, the connectivity, the additional e-mails . . . it's more complicated to keep up and to track information. So we need to work even harder to keep simplifying."

In most situations, companies don't really have a choice about keeping at it. ConAgra Foods is a case in point. As described in chapter 1, Gary Rodkin made simplicity a rallying cry and a business imperative after he became CEO late in 2005. In the next eighteen months, he and his leadership team proceeded to restructure the company, rationalize the product portfolio, rewire many of the processes, and build simplicity into the management culture— all with great success and widespread employee engagement. By most measures, victory was at hand.

But then complexity—both internally and externally generated—began to flood back: a manufacturing problem in a plant caused a recall of a key peanut butter product; industry research accelerated the need to reformulate the way popcorn was produced; problems with a tomato harvest caused supply delays for key customers; labeling concerns caused another recall; and commodity prices such as oil and wheat suddenly spiked to record levels, far beyond any projections. At the same time, a couple of important senior managers decided to leave the company, and the responsibilities of the leadership team had to be redistributed.

As Rodkin and his team scrambled to deal with all these issues, it became clear to them that many of the basic processes for running the company were too slow, complex, and cumbersome for such a fast-paced, crisis-driven environment: financial forecasting, pricing, cost-of-goods management, SKU birthing, quality assurance, and many others. With this realization—and the need to further reduce costs in the face of changing business conditions— Rodkin and the senior leadership team initiated another wave of simplification efforts. Rodkin observed: "We made such good progress the first couple of years that perhaps we got overconfident. Then the environment reminded us of how much more work there was to do. The key is to not stop—simplicity is an ongoing battle." The point, of course, is that simplification is never over, finished, or complete.

Pete Perez, ConAgra's head of human resources, thinks that in the long run, building increased capacity for ongoing change and process streamlining will be the most important aspect of his company's simplification work: "From the very beginning, we set out to build simplification into the neighborhoods of the company, and not just have a few people drive it from the center. That's why we've trained transformation leaders, RoadMap facilitators, streamline teams, and many of our managers in process-simplification tools— and built it into our expectations for how we work with each other. We're not all the way there yet, but we've got a strong foundation to build upon."

So it really is possible to lead a comprehensive attack on complexity and to make progress both in the short term and over the long haul. If you are a senior executive, or lead a division or function, or consult to someone who does, then the five steps presented here will give you a picture of what might be involved.

Of course, not everyone is in position to lead a comprehensive, multiyear simplification initiative. But even if you're not, you still don't need to wait for someone else to take the lead. You can do a lot, in your own job and sphere of influence, to combat complexity and make life simpler and more productive for yourself, your colleagues, and your customers. Read on for some ways to get started.

SEVEN

Simplicity Starts with You

E VERYONE IS FAMILIAR WITH THE term KISS: "Keep it simple, Stupid." It's a trite and overused phrase and may not seem to belong in a serious business book. But if you are in a position of leadership—whether of an entire company, a division, a function, a team, or a project—that's your challenge: how do you keep things simple in the face of the complexities arrayed against you?

You certainly face a lot of complexities, stemming as they do from structural mitosis, product proliferation, process evolution, and your own behavior and that of your colleagues, and it's clear that the job will never be finished. Even with an action framework for combating complexity over the long haul, it may be tempting to think that making things simpler is a complex undertaking, one better left to someone else. But that would be a mistake.

Simplification doesn't have to be complex. It doesn't have to be difficult. You can do a lot today and the next day to make your organization simpler for yourself, your colleagues, and your customers—even if you're not the CEO and aren't positioned to lead a comprehensive, multiyear strategy for simplification. There's no need to wait. You can get started now, simply and quickly.

If Not You, Who?

If you're waiting for someone else to initiate simplification, you might have to wait a long time. Sure, some enlightened and forward-looking CEOs do make it their business to drive simplification efforts. But for every Jeffrey Immelt and Annika Falkengren and Gary Rodkin, hundreds of others soldier on without recognizing the quagmire of complexity that surrounds them or understanding how they are contributing to the problem. Even those who do see complexity around them often don't know what to do. If you work for or with one of these managers, you might as well buy a lottery ticket. Your chances of being pulled into a simpler world are about the same as hitting the jackpot—unless you do something about it.

My colleague Robert Schaffer sums up the situation this way: most managers act as though they live in a box—a box that limits what they can do. Obviously, part of the box is determined by official limits set out in job descriptions, hierarchical arrangements, and formal work rules. But a large part of the box, perhaps even most of it, is self-created and self-imposed. We work within our comfort zones, doing what we think we should do or what we think other people want us to do. But most of the time, we don't question, challenge, or test those limits, which makes them self-perpetuating.

Here are some common examples:

- How many times have you gone to a meeting that lacked an agenda, had no clear set of objectives, was poorly led, and seemed unlikely to generate clear outcomes and next steps—but didn't do anything about it?

- How often have you received unnecessary e-mails or reports that you didn't need to see—but didn't let the senders know that the messages were clogging up your inbox?

- How often have you sat through a presentation with too many slides, unclear points, and too much data—but didn't provide feedback to the presenter?

- How often have you taken on an assignment or a project without a clear goal, a specific time frame, or measurable outcomes—but just accepted the confusion as business as usual?

- How often have you listened to complaints from customers and colleagues about processes that took too long or didn't make sense—but you didn't take any action to fix the underlying problem?

- How often have you participated in company-wide activities like budgeting and strategic planning, thinking that there had to be a better way—but didn't share your ideas with anyone else?

- How often have you thought to yourself that your company's products or services were too complicated or too numerous or not user-friendly—but just accepted these complexities as a normal way of doing business?

In the late 1960s, it was common to say that if you were not part of the solution, you were part of the problem.[1] It still applies, and it especially applies to organizational simplification. We often assume that things are as they are and that we cannot influence or change them. But why not try to make things simpler and better and faster? If you don't start to simplify, who else will?

After all, organizations are complex social systems. They combine the strengths and the weaknesses of hundreds or thousands—or hundreds of thousands—of people. In the face of this complexity, it is easy to feel that the actions of one person won't make much difference. As one manager put it, "It's like spitting in the ocean." But accepting this explanation (or excuse) for inaction is part of an unconscious collusion that perpetuates and amplifies complexity. The more you accept complexity and do nothing about it, the worse it becomes. On the other hand, if you push the needle in the other direction, even by simplifying small things under your control, you will influence others to join you and your impact will be multiplied many times over.

To prove it works, here's a look at a couple of managers who took this approach.

Taking the Initiative to Simplify

When "Terry Davis" joined the "ABC Clinical Software" division as the unit's first vice president of operations in July 2007, his job definition was somewhat open-ended and amorphous.[2] His organization is a leading provider of clinical software solutions for hospital care teams—helping hospitals integrate clinical information more effectively. Like many software companies, ABC works hard to balance its support for existing customers with the development of new applications—both of which involve the same software development and customer service teams. Terry's assignment was to look at how this system operated from end to end and to identify areas of improvement for its customers.

Within a few days, Terry began to see the real reason he'd been hired: almost everyone he spoke to was feeling overwhelmed. Clinical software in hospitals is mission critical, and problems with it undercut patient care. So the first priority at ABC was to support existing applications, many of which had been acquired from other firms and linked together to work with other hospital systems. Keeping it all running effectively often required particular skills that were in short supply. As a result, the development professionals were constantly being pulled from one project to another and didn't feel that they were getting any of their projects done in the time they hoped. At the same time, customer teams were working on-site to install or update applications, and the teams often ran into problems that required consultation from the same developers. And, of course, the developers were supposed to be working on new applications and products, so shifting priorities risked delaying the new software's release dates. Exacerbating these dynamics was the reality that ABC had grown quickly, partly through acquisitions, and was still on the learning curve to mature and standardized processes.

Combined, these issues put enormous pressure on the organization. To get all the work done, management wanted to hire and train more developers—but couldn't hire enough, because it had to hold the line on expenses. At the same time, it was constantly reacting to urgent customer problems, dealing with a stressed-out workforce and struggling, as most software companies do, to launch its new products. It wasn't a pretty picture.

In the face of this complexity, Terry realized that creating metrics and operational models alone wouldn't be enough. At best, the metrics would further illuminate the problems; they wouldn't solve them. At worst, additional metrics would make people feel even more overloaded and frustrated—and would brand him as a corporate bureaucrat rather than someone who could help, especially in the eyes of developers, who certainly didn't want any more reports to fill out, or his senior colleagues, who were groaning under the administrative burden they already had.

Terry was fresh from another management job (at a major food retail chain), where he'd met similar operational complexity. He had done some research about Six Sigma and Work-Out, and he liked the idea of engaging people closest to the work to jointly solve problems, rather than telling them what to do. But his efforts there weren't valued, and he hadn't been able to make any progress. Given the situation at ABC, he decided to try again. He was sure that one of the keys to improvement would be to identify and eliminate unnecessary or low-value-added work that the developers were doing—which would give them more time both for customer issues and for new product development.

But how do you get a work-simplification effort started across a company when you're not the CEO, nobody has given you a mandate, and none of the people who would need to be involved actually report to you? That was Terry's problem. To solve it, he decided to assume that he did have a mandate in the context of being the new operations vice president, and that he could define his role accordingly, at least until someone told him otherwise. And with that mindset, Terry began to talk to his fellow managers and their people about their ideas for operational improvement and to educate them about approaches such as Work-Out and Six Sigma. Within a couple of weeks, he had collected a long list of opportunities—and also created a buzz about the possibility that things might change. In fact, as the word spread that Terry was going to address the overload and process problems, people came to him personally and started to send him unsolicited e-mail with even more ideas.

Armed with the list of opportunities, Terry won agreement from his boss to run a couple of pilot Work-Outs with help from one of my colleagues. Terry then asked a senior management associate who had expressed support for his efforts to cosponsor the first sessions. But then reality intruded. The company was in the midst of an intense drive to improve its cost structure, and Terry had to make sure that Work-Out wasn't viewed as just another vehicle for reducing the head count. So Terry decided to slow down and further educate his colleagues and employees about how eliminating low-value work and simplifying processes would be beneficial both for the cost structure and for everyone's quality of work life—especially since the demands from customers and for meeting the new release schedule would not diminish. Since people were already struggling to keep up, things would only get worse unless they did something about it. To reinforce this message, Terry created a set of operational rules of the road, as shown in figure 7-1.

Using these rules of the road as a starting point, Terry initiated the first Work-Out session, in December 2007. Thirty-five people from development, customer service, and functional areas spent a day brainstorming ways of saving time and then made specific recommendations to Terry and the manager of customer support. Together, they approved ideas for simplifying the password-reset process, reducing requests for information in service operations, streamlining the time-recording process for domestic contractors, reducing time for preparation and review of service agreements,

FIGURE 7-1

Terry Davis's operational rules of the road

and many others. Participants then signed on for implementation and tracking—to make sure that the changes really stuck and that the estimated five thousand hours of time savings were realized. Most important, people now felt that management was starting to do something about the chaotic workload and lack of simple processes. Terry's message was getting through.

As word of the first Work-Out circulated throughout the company, demand for it started to increase. One midlevel manager who had participated in the first Work-Out saw the potential to go even further in customer support; he convinced his boss to sponsor an additional session just for her group. As interest grew, Terry then went back to his original list of process-simplification ideas and asked the senior team to support the work. He got the team's agreement to train internal people to design and facilitate Work-Outs, and over the next several months, the consultants trained six designers and eleven facilitators who could lead Work-Outs internally. The consultants and internal people then collaborated to design and conduct simplification Work-Outs on two major processes—error messaging and 24/7 availability of key systems environments. Terry then developed a method and plan for continuing the efforts into the next year so that a new process would be tackled every month or so—with an overall goal of eliminating at least fifty thousand hours of wasted time. Plans also were under way for engaging a key hospital customer in a joint simplification effort. Not a bad impact for a guy with an amorphous job and no mandate to drive simplification.

Everyone Can Be a Terry Davis

The lesson from Terry Davis's experience is that you don't have to be a CEO to drive simplicity in your organization. You don't even need a formal assignment or formal authority. You can build on your own energy, your own ability to raise questions, and your own initiative to make things happen. Most people in organizations want simplicity—it's not a hard sell. If you can help them understand how they can get better results while also making their lives easier, they'll listen. And if you can move them into action, you'll be a hero. The only limitation is you—your own definition of the box around your job. Expand the box. Expand the impact.

Here's another quick example: Mieko Nishimizu retired in 2004 as vice president of the South Asia Region of The World Bank. A Japanese national trained in economics, Mieko began her career as an academic before joining The World Bank in 1980. After a series of technical assessment and financial advisory assignments, Mieko was appointed country director for several countries in South Asia in 1995, and regional vice president in 1997.[3]

When Mieko first became a country manager, she realized that while poverty reduction was her mission, she didn't really understand what this meant from the perspective of her customers, the people who lived in the countries. She could do the intellectual analysis of per-capita incomes and macroeconomic health, but that brought her no closer to understanding the day-to-day lives of the people she was supposed to be helping. And without that underlying emotional understanding, the programs, policies, and products that she and her team developed were likely to be off the mark. She needed a simpler and more direct line of sight to her clientele.

As a result of this insight, Mieko spent six weeks living in a remote area of Pakistan with rural villagers. She later described it as a "mind-boggling experience": "I went in with the mind-set of an economist and came out as something else. I learned about the wisdom of poor people, what they do to control their lives and expand their horizons. And I saw the World Bank through their eyes."

Two years later, when Mieko became regional vice president, she encouraged her staff to have this same experience. It became known as the "village immersion program," in which World Bank professionals would spend two weeks living the lives of the poor in their villages with support from local nongovernmental organizations. Eventually, Mieko made the program mandatory for certain categories of her staff, with more than two hundred people participating over the course of a few years. Soon other regions in the bank picked up on the program as well.

The impact of Mieko's simple initiative was profound. As she describes it:

> The traditional Western colonial mentality is that "we" know better about how to provide assistance. But the experience of living with poor people wiped away that notion. We don't know better. Our clients need us to be humble, to listen to them deeply, to understand their needs, and to holistically help them to solve their own problems . . . Otherwise we end up building a girls' school without bathrooms, or setting up agricultural extension services without roads.

According to Mieko, the village immersion program "sent an enormous signal about the attitude of the World Bank to listen and learn, rather than dictate and impose."

Nobody asked Mieko to shift the perspective of The World Bank and its professional staff to be more directly client-centered. Nobody gave her the assignment of refocusing the bank's lending and technical assistance products so that they would be more simply aimed at clients' needs. Mieko expanded her own world and her own sense of initiative. She enlarged the box around herself and created a model for many others.

Opportunities for Impact

Once you accept the idea of taking the initiative to drive simplicity—from whatever position you hold—what can you do? What steps can you take to enlarge the box around you and make simplification more of a reality in your organization? Here are five simple ideas:

- Hold up a mirror.

- Present a business case.

- Stimulate fresh thinking—from the outside in.

- Build a coalition.

- Demonstrate that simplicity makes a difference.

Hold Up a Mirror

Much of the complexity in organizations is unconscious and unintentional. We tend to accept it and learn to live with it, and after a while, we don't even see it anymore. That's why a mirror is a powerful tool—it helps people see things about themselves that they can't see on their own.

The diagnostic instruments included in this book, particularly the questionnaire in chapter 1, will help you hold up a mirror to your organization and help people see the complexity they have been taking for granted. Just remember that the instruments alone are not sufficient; they need to be coupled with dialogue and discussion. Otherwise, people will only be looking at tiny bits of the mirror, which can give a distorted picture. You need to get a number of people, perhaps from different functions or levels, to add all their perspectives. Combining the views will give you a clearer picture.

Present a Business Case

While complexity is often annoying and uncomfortable, the real reason for attacking it has to be rooted in business results and outcomes. Otherwise, simplicity will remain a value to aspire to, rather than a real driver of change and improvement. The leaders I've described here have understood this and declared simplicity a business imperative. But you don't have to be the CEO to highlight the business rationale for simplification. All managers (and employees) can do it for their own areas or from their own perspectives.

Of course, you can make the business case for simplicity in many ways. You can do a quantitative time analysis of how long it takes you and your colleagues to complete a key business process—and reveal the savings you would reap if you eliminated unnecessary steps. You can do a similar analysis of how you and your colleagues spend a typical day—focusing on how much time is spent on mission-critical tasks and how much on low-value or non-value-added activities. You also can do a comparative analysis of your performance versus the competition's—how long it takes your company to sell (or install or price or resolve or answer) compared with how long it takes a competitor to do the same. You can look at the costs associated with product complexity and SKU proliferation, as illustrated in the Aeron chair example in chapter 3.

The point is that you need to create a compelling context for why simplicity is important and how it will make a difference. If you want to get people's attention, show them where the money is, or where the money should be.

Stimulate Fresh Thinking—from the Outside In

Remember the importance of designing your organization, your products, and your processes with your customers in mind. Simplicity often directly correlates with your ability to align with what your customers want, when they want it, and how they want it. That doesn't mean that you can't influence your customers or provide them with innovations they haven't thought of themselves. But you need to at least start with your customers' perspective so that your innovation will be rooted in their reality.

Except for salespeople, customer service representatives, and a few senior executives, most people in organizations have no regular direct contact with customers. It's easy, therefore, to get insular, to think from the inside out instead of the outside in. So it's useful to bring the customer perspective to the forefront—and you have many opportunities to do so, whatever the position you hold in your company. And you don't have to go live in a village in Pakistan to do it. For example:

- Invite a customer to one of your team meetings.

- Take your team to visit a customer site.

- Spend a couple of hours listening in on phone calls with your service representatives, either live or taped.

- Ask each of your people to interview a customer, and then have a discussion to review what was learned.

- Solicit feedback and ideas from customers through electronic questionnaires, social networks, and online community interest groups.

And you can do all of these things, and many others, with internal customers as well as business-to-business or end-use customers. The only limitation is your own creativity—and the constraints of the box that you place around yourself and your team. But if you do these things on a regular basis, it will almost certainly spark fresh thinking about how to design your work (or your products or services) more simply.

Build a Coalition

You can certainly have an impact on your organization by modeling simplification in your own area. Other managers will take notice and your innovations may spread organically, like Mieko's village immersion program at The World Bank. To have even greater impact, however, you can intentionally build a coalition of like-minded managers to share ideas and best practices and to jointly address systemic complexity. To a large extent, that was Terry Davis's approach at ABC. He didn't have a mandate on his own, but by making the rounds of other managers and staff, he found colleagues who were willing to join him. Representing this coalition made it easier for him to secure the backing of his boss and to procure budget for consulting. It also accelerated the multiplication of simplification activities as other managers picked up the ball for their own areas and were willing to participate in efforts that crossed functional lines.

Building a coalition for simplification, however, doesn't need to be done only through a series of one-on-one meetings. Today's social technologies can be powerful vehicles for creating interest in simplification, getting rapid feedback, testing ideas, and propagating experiments.[4] A number of companies, such as Intuitive Surgical in Sunnyvale, California, are encouraging their people to create and join in-house social networks that can serve as forums for discussion of key topics such as product or process complexity. Cisco Systems uses its intranet to engage its own employees in discussions of marketing strategies and tactics, as well as to solicit ideas and get feedback on them. Another high-tech company uses an in-house site similar to YouTube to share two-minute video examples of employee simplification initiatives. Intel created an internal wiki called Intelpedia that has thousands of employee-generated entries to help people navigate all kinds of technical and organizational issues.[5] Many companies also are using blogs, virtual sites (such as Second Life), YouTube, and various external social networking sites to actively bring people together, including customers. Undoubtedly, as more people who have grown up with these technologies and ways of connecting enter the workforce, these technological tools will become even more prominent opportunities for building coalitions.

Demonstrate That Simplicity Makes a Difference

Perhaps implicit in the first four tactics is the idea that you actually have to do something. Simplicity is great to talk about. Most people find it cathartic to share their complexity war stories. But nothing builds momentum for simplification as much as real success. If you're looking for one takeaway from this book, this is it: *the way to make things simpler in your organization is to start simplifying.* Just do it. Learn from your experience, and do it again. Ultimately, all the tactics, strategies, and plans come down to this: take action, get some initial results, and build on success. Do it on your own, or do it with your team, or do it with colleagues. But really do it.

This book is meant to be 10 percent inspirational and 90 percent perspirational (if there is such a word). Fighting through complexity and creating a simpler organization is hard work. The floods of complexity—economic, social, technological, and psychological—continue unabated. And it is human nature to unintentionally and unconsciously exacerbate and amplify complexity. If it were easy, every organization would be simple. Who wouldn't want it that way? But in spite of everything, simplification is possible if you're willing to get started. Simplify a presentation. Streamline a process. Focus your service offerings. Make your assignments or instructions easier to read. Reduce your e-mail volume. Start where you have some control and can make a difference, and then keep going.

The core of this book—the chapters on structural mitosis, product proliferation, process evolution, and managerial behavior—offers an extensive toolkit for simplification. For easy reference, these tools and approaches (which were first introduced in chapter 1) are listed here again as a reminder (table 7-1). Use these

TABLE 7-1

Road map for simplicity

	Causes of complexity	Approaches for increasing simplicity
Structural mitosis	• Focusing on structure before strategy • Designing based on people and personalities • Building mechanical rather than organic organizations	• Differentiate between core and context • Take a customer perspective • Consolidate similar functions and tasks • Prune layers, and increase spans of control
Product proliferation	• Volume complexity • Support complexity • System complexity • Design complexity	• Portfolio analysis • SKU rationalization and reduction • Customer design partnering
Process evolution	• Local differences • Multiplication of steps and loops • Informality of process • Lack of cross-functional or cross-unit transparency	• Best-practice identification • Process mapping and redesign • Six Sigma and Lean • Rapid results • Work-Out
Managerial behavior	• Overdoing strengths • Avoiding areas of discomfort	• *Strategy, planning, and budgeting:* Decide how much detail is enough • *Goal setting and demand making:* Improve calibration, and avoid the seven deadly sins • *Communications:* Clarify message and who needs to receive it

tools as appropriate, either to get started and demonstrate early results, or as part of a more comprehensive strategy over time.

As a way of selecting which tool to use, consider the variables pictured in figure 7-2.[6] What is the business result that needs to be achieved? What type of complexity needs to be tackled in order to achieve that result, and what is the cause of the complexity? Which tool or approach best addresses this cause of complexity? What leadership can you or others bring to bear in moving forward? By aligning your personal simplification strategy around the answers

FIGURE 7-2

Developing a personal simplification strategy: Variables to consider

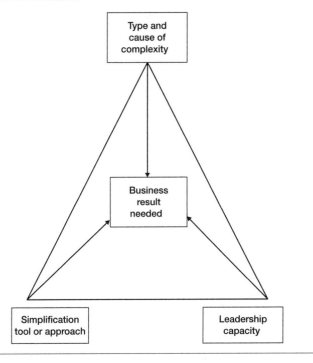

to these questions, you can construct a powerful, tailored way of getting started and of expanding the box around your job and your career. And if you don't take the lead in doing this, who will?

Simplicity-Minded Management: The Next Frontier

Every manager—CEO, division president, functional leader, supervisor, or team leader—has the capacity to simplify. Most likely, it's not in your job description or part of the leadership competencies of your firm. But it should be—and you should put it there, front and center. As Gary Rodkin of ConAgra Foods puts it, "Simplification is the next frontier of productivity."

Every organization—for-profit or nonprofit, private or public—is in business to get things done. If you can accomplish your mission with fewer steps, clearer processes, greater customer alignment, and less wasted motion, then you will be at a competitive advantage in our increasingly complex, global, and fast-changing world. To do that, you need to expand the box around your job, redefining your role and scope of authority. Hold the mirror up to the organization. Make the business case for simplification. Encourage an external perspective. Build a coalition. And demonstrate results. And then do it over and over again.

If you take these simple steps, the results might not be perfect. But you will gradually expand your box, and your colleagues will notice. You will have an influence and an impact beyond your formal role. Your career might evolve in ways that you can't imagine. You might even start a movement and a revolution in your company. But even if your aspirations are more modest, whatever you do will help give your organization a better chance of surviving and thriving in the complex world of the twenty-first century.

Simplicity starts with you.

NOTES

Preface

1. Ron Ashkenas, "Simplicity-Minded Management," *Harvard Business Review,* December 2007.

2. Jenny Anderson and Heather Timmons, "Why a U.S. Subprime Mortgage Crisis Is Felt Around the World," *New York Times*, August 31, 2007, www.nytimes.com/2007/08/31/business/worldbusiness/31derivatives.html.

3. Thomas Friedman, *The World Is Flat* (New York: Farrar, Straus and Giroux, 2005); Alvin Toffler, *Future Shock* (New York: Bantam Press, 1984).

4. "Dilbert on How to Save Your Career," *Fortune* Magazine online, http://askannie.blogs.fortune.cnn.com/2008/12/11/dilbert-on-how-to-save-your-career/.

Chapter 1

1. See John C. Bogle, *Enough: True Measures of Money, Business, and Life* (New York: John Wiley, 2008).

2. See Margaret J. Wheatley, *Leadership and the New Science: Discovering Order in a Chaotic World*, 3rd ed. (San Francisco: Berrett-Koehler, 2006).

3. For a discussion of common management fads, see Ron Ashkenas, "Beyond the Fads: How Leaders Drive Change with Results," in *Managing Strategic and Cultural Change in Organizations*, ed. C. Schneier (Chicago: Human Resource Planning Society, 1995).

4. Bill Jensen, *Simplicity: The New Competitive Advantage in a World of More, Better, Faster* (New York: Perseus, 2000).

Chapter 2

1. "Industrial Autocracy and the Workingman," *New York Times*, March 16, 1919 (from archives).

2. For a more detailed discussion of the organization as a living organism rather than as a mechanical construction, see Margaret J. Wheatley, *Leadership and the New Science: Learning About Organization from an Orderly Universe* (San Francisco: Berrett-Koehler, 1992). Also see Ron Ashkenas, Dave Ulrich, Todd Jick, and Steve Kerr, *The Boundaryless Organization*, 2nd ed. (San Francisco: Jossey-Bass, 2002).

3. Geoffrey Moore, *Dealing with Darwin: How Great Companies Innovate at Every Phase of Their Evolution* (New York: HarperCollins, 2005).

4. Information about the Office of the Future is based on the author's interview with Jordan Cohen, and from the following article: Arianne Cohen, "Scuttling Scut Work," *Fast Company*, February 2008, 42–43.

5. George Hattrup and Brian H. Kleiner, "How to Establish the Proper Span of Control for Managers," *Industrial Management*, November–December 1993.

6. Arlene Weintraub, "Can Pfizer Prime the Pipeline?" *BusinessWeek*, December 31, 2007–January 7, 2008, 90–91.

7. Lew Trecarten, "Lindex: An Organizational Layering Index," *Optimum* 21.1 (1990–1991): 52–67.

Chapter 3

1. The team included Zurich people as well as consultants from the Dutch marketing firm VODW, which could provide an external, objective perspective.

2. Further information on this case is found in Robert Schaffer and Ron Ashkenas, *Rapid Results: How 100-Day Projects Build the Capacity for Large-Scale Change* (New York: Jossey-Bass, 2005), 188–189.

3. John Graham, "The iPod As a Business Model," *Air Conditioning, Heating, and Refrigeration News*, February 12, 2007, 16.

4. Linda Tischler, "The Beauty of Simplicity," *Fast Company*, December 19, 2007.

5. Ibid.

6. See Tom Kelly, *The Art of Innovation: Lessons in Creativity from IDEO, America's Leading Design Firm* (New York: Doubleday, 2001).

7. John Maeda, *The Laws of Simplicity: Design, Technology, Business, Life* (Cambridge, MA: MIT Press, 2006).

8. Evolution of GE's retailer financial services business through 2002 is described in Ron Ashkenas, Dave Ulrich, Todd Jick, and Steve Kerr, *The Boundaryless Organization*, 2nd ed. (San Francisco: Jossey-Bass, 2002).

9. Case provided by Richard Lesser and Amyn Merchant of BCG and used with their permission.

10. The Designs of the Decade: Best in Business 1990–1999 Awards competition was sponsored by the Industrial Designers Society of America (IDSA) and *BusinessWeek* magazine. For the 2002 award, see "The 15 Best Product Designs," *Fast Company*, June 2002.

11. From Herman Miller online product showroom, www.hermanmiller.com.

12. For further information about how Cisco uses customer input to get ahead of technology trends, see Bronwyn Fryer and Tom Stewart, "Cisco Sees the Future: Interview with John Chambers," *Harvard Business Review*, November 2008, 72–79.

Chapter 4

1. Christopher Bartlett and Sumantra Ghoshal, *Managing Across Borders* (Boston: Harvard Business School Press, 1989).

2. Ron Ashkenas, Dave Ulrich, Todd Jick, and Steve Kerr, *The Boundaryless Organization: Breaking the Chains of Organizational Structure*, 2nd ed. (San Francisco: Jossey-Bass, 2002), 259.

3. Dave Ulrich, Steve Kerr, and Ron Ashkenas, *The GE Work-Out* (New York: McGraw-Hill, 2002), 153.

4. Ron Ashkenas, Lawrence DeMonaco, and Suzanne Francis, "Making the Deal Real: How GE Capital Integrates Acquisitions," *Harvard Business Review*, January–February 1998, 165–178.

5. For further information on best-practice identification and sharing, see Jac Fitz-Enz, *The 8 Practices of Exceptional Companies: How Great Organizations Make the Most of Their Human Assets* (New York: AMACOM Division American Management Assn., 2005); and Stephen Denning, *The Secret Language of Leadership: How Leaders Inspire Action Through Narrative* (San Francisco: Jossey Bass, 2007).

6. For further information on process mapping and redesign, see M. Hammer and J. Champy, *Reengineering the Corporation: A Manifesto for Business Revolution* (New York: Harper Business, 2001); and Ron Ashkenas, Todd Jick, Dave Ulrich, and Catherine Paul-Chowdhury, *The Boundaryless Organization Field Guide* (San Francisco: Jossey-Bass, 1998).

7. For further information, see Rath & Strong, *Rath & Strong's Six Sigma Leadership Handbook*, ed. T. Bertels (New York: John Wiley and Sons, 2003).

8. Robert Schaffer and Ron Ashkenas, *Rapid Results: How 100-Day Projects Build the Capacity for Large-Scale Change* (San Francisco: Jossey-Bass, 2005). See also Patrice Murphy, Celia Kirwan, and Ron Ashkenas, "Rapid Results," in *The Change Handbook*, 2nd ed., eds. Peggy Holman, Tom Devane, and Steven Cady (San Francisco: Berrett-Koehler, 2007), 450–464.

9. Nadim Matta and Ron Ashkenas, "Why Good Projects Fail Anyway," *Harvard Business Review*, September 2003.

10. For further information, see Ulrich, Kerr, and Ashkenas, *GE Work-Out*.

11. Ron Ashkenas, Matthew McCreight, and Patrice Murphy, "Work-Out and Six Sigma," in *Rath & Strong's Six Sigma Handbook*, ed. T. Bertels (New York: J. Wiley and Sons, 2003).

Chapter 5

1. Bob Kaplan and Rob Kaiser, *The Versatile Leader* (San Francisco: Jossey-Bass, 2006).

2. For a more extensive discussion of this psychological dynamic, see Ron Ashkenas and Robert Schaffer, "Managers Can Avoid Wasting Time," *Harvard Business Review*, May–June 1982, 98–104.

3. Robert Kaplan and Robert Kaiser, "Stop Overdoing Your Strengths," *Harvard Business Review*, February 2009.

4. Henry Mintzberg, "Crafting Strategy," *Harvard Business Review*, July–August 1987, 66–75.

5. Jeffrey Pfeffer and Robert Sutton, *The Knowing-Doing Gap: How Smart Companies Turn Knowledge into Action* (Boston: Harvard Business School Press, 2000).

6. Robert Schaffer, "Demand Better Results—and Get Them," *Harvard Business Review*, November–December 1974 (reissued and revised March–April 1991).

7. Morgan McCall, *High Flyers: Developing the Next Generation of Leaders* (Boston: Harvard Business School Press, 1998).

8. Kaplan and Kaiser, *The Versatile Leader.*

9. For further discussion of planning disciplines and why managers avoid them, see Robert Neiman, *Execution Plain and Simple: Twelve Steps to Achieving Any Goal on Time and on Budget* (New York: McGraw-Hill, 2004).

10. David J. Collis and Michael G. Rukstad, "Can You Say What Your Strategy Is?" *Harvard Business Review*, April 2008, 82–90.

11. John Cleese, *Meetings, Bloody Meetings* (John Cleese Business Training Videos, 1993).

12. For a fuller description of the changes Wolfensohn initiated, see S. Mallaby, *The World's Banker* (New York: Penguin Press, 2004).

Chapter 6

1. This case is based on interviews with GE executives Mark Begor, John Lynch, Susan Peters, and Lloyd Trotter as well as personal observation.

2. Jack Welch, *Jack: Straight From the Gut* (New York: Warner Business Books, 2001).

3. Dave Ulrich, Steve Kerr, and Ron Ashkenas, "GE's Leadership Work-Out," *Leader to Leader* (Spring 2002).

4. This case is based on interviews with Annika Falkengren and Viveka Hirdman-Ryrberg.

5. Steve Kerr, "On the Folly of Rewarding A While Asking for B," *Academy of Management Journal* (1975): 769–783. See also Steve Kerr, *Reward Systems: Does Yours Measure Up?* (Boston: Harvard Business Press, 2009).

Chapter 7

1. This phrase was first coined by my friend Charlie Rosner as part of an advertising campaign for Vista, the government's domestic community service organization, in 1968.

2. The case described here is real, but the manager and company have been disguised.

3. This case is based on an interview with Mieko Nishimizu, in Ron Ashkenas, Dave Ulrich, Todd Jick, and Steve Kerr, *The Boundaryless Organization*, 2nd ed. (San Francisco: Jossey-Bass, 2002), 243–246.

4. For a complete discussion of how social technologies can be used to build coalitions, see Charlene Li and Josh Bernoff, *Groundswell: Winning in a World Transformed by Social Technologies* (Boston: Harvard Business Press, 2008).

5. Ibid., 223. A *wiki* is a Web site that is open to modification (corrections, additions, or other changes) by the participants.

6. Thanks to Rizwan Khan at the Vanguard Group, for his assistance with this framework.

INDEX

Ron Ashkenas is a Managing Partner of Robert H. Schaffer & Associates in Stamford, Connecticut; and an internationally recognized consultant and speaker on organizational transformation, leadership, and postmerger integration.

Since joining RHS&A in the late-1970s, Ron has helped dozens of organizations achieve dramatic performance improvements while strengthening their leadership capacity. He is a highly valued consultant and coach to CEOs and senior executives who want to accelerate the pace of change. He also works with staff groups and internal consultants to strengthen the bottom-line impact of their professional contributions. Ron's clients value his pragmatic approach and insight into their challenges as well as his ability to help them navigate and overcome the political and psychological obstacles that so often threaten success.

Ron was part of the original team that collaborated with then-CEO Jack Welch to develop GE's Work-Out approach, which constituted one of the largest and most successful corporate transformations in history. Since then, Ron has led RHS&A's efforts to adapt and enhance the Work-Out methodology and apply it to other organizations.

Among Ron's clients are many *Fortune* 500 companies, as well as financial, governmental, and nonprofit organizations, including

JP MorganChase, Cisco Systems, the Federal Reserve Bank of New York, Pfizer, the World Bank, GlaxoSmithKline, Johnson & Johnson, ArvinMeritor Automotive, Zurich Financial Services, ConAgra Foods, and the Stanford University Hospitals and Clinics.

Ron has published dozens of articles and book chapters. Five of his articles have appeared in *Harvard Business Review*, including "Making the Deal Real: How GE Capital Integrates Acquisitions" and "Why Good Projects Fail Anyway." Others have appeared in the *National Productivity Review*, the *Human Resource Management Journal*, and *Leader to Leader*. Ron is the coauthor of three previous books: *The Boundaryless Organization* (Jossey-Bass, 1995, and 2nd edition in 2002), with Dave Ulrich, Todd Jick, and Steve Kerr; *The GE Work-Out* (McGraw-Hill, 2002), with Ulrich and Kerr; and *Rapid Results!* (Jossey-Bass, 2005), with Robert Schaffer and other members of RHS&A.

Ron lectures and offers seminars on organizational transformation and postmerger integration worldwide. He has been on the faculty of executive education programs at major universities including Stanford Business School, the Kellogg School at Northwestern, and the Weatherhead School of Management at Case Western Reserve.

Ron received his BA from Wesleyan University, his EdM from Harvard University, and his PhD in organizational behavior from Case Western Reserve University. He and his wife Barbara have three grown children and one fast-growing grandchild and reside in Stamford, Connecticut. He can be reached at Ron@rhsa.com.